TABLE OF CONTENTS

MATH

PRACTICE WORKBOOK

{ALGEBRA}

+ guided practice questions

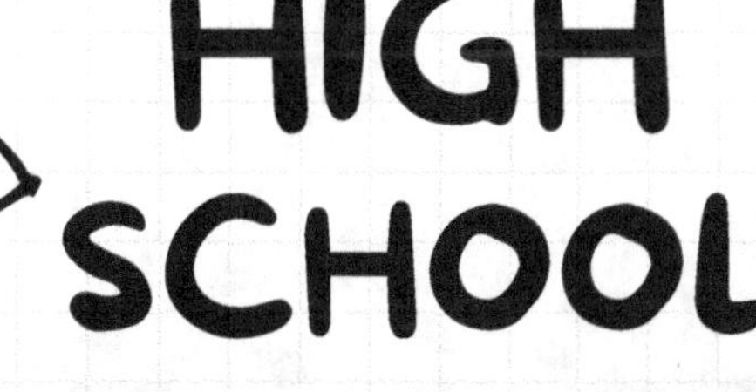

2000+ QUESTIONS
YOU NEED TO KILL IN ⇒ HIGH SCHOOL

 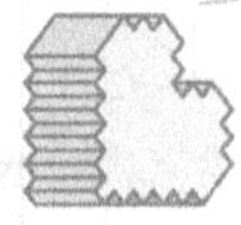

Books made by **Brain Hunter Prep** with love from New York

GRADE 1-3

GRADE 4-5

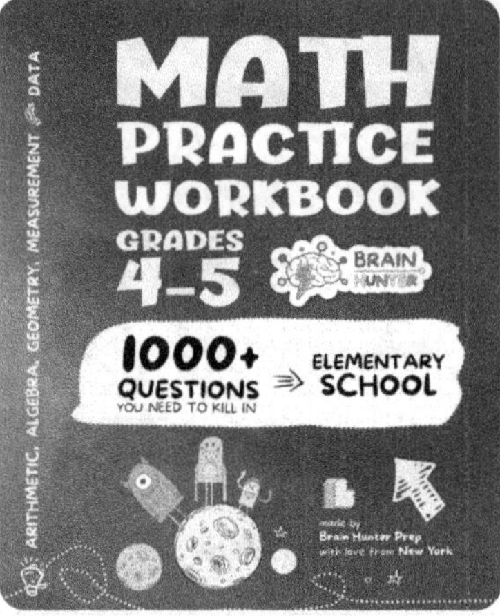

GRADE 6-8

KIDS SUMMER ACADEMY SERIES

ArgoPrep's **Kids Summer Academy** series helps prevent summer learning loss and gets students ready for their new school year by reinforcing core foundations in math, english and science. Our workbooks also introduce new concepts so students can get a head start and be on top of their game for the new school year!

INTRODUCING MATH!

Introducing Math! by ArgoPrep is an award-winning series created by certified teachers to provide students with high-quality practice problems. Our workbooks include topic overviews with instruction, practice questions, answer explanations along with digital access to video explanations. Practice in confidence - with ArgoPrep!

SCIENCE SERIES

Science Daily Practice Workbook by ArgoPrep is an award-winning series created by certified science teachers to help build mastery of foundational science skills. Our workbooks explore science topics in depth with ArgoPrep's 5 E's to build science mastery.

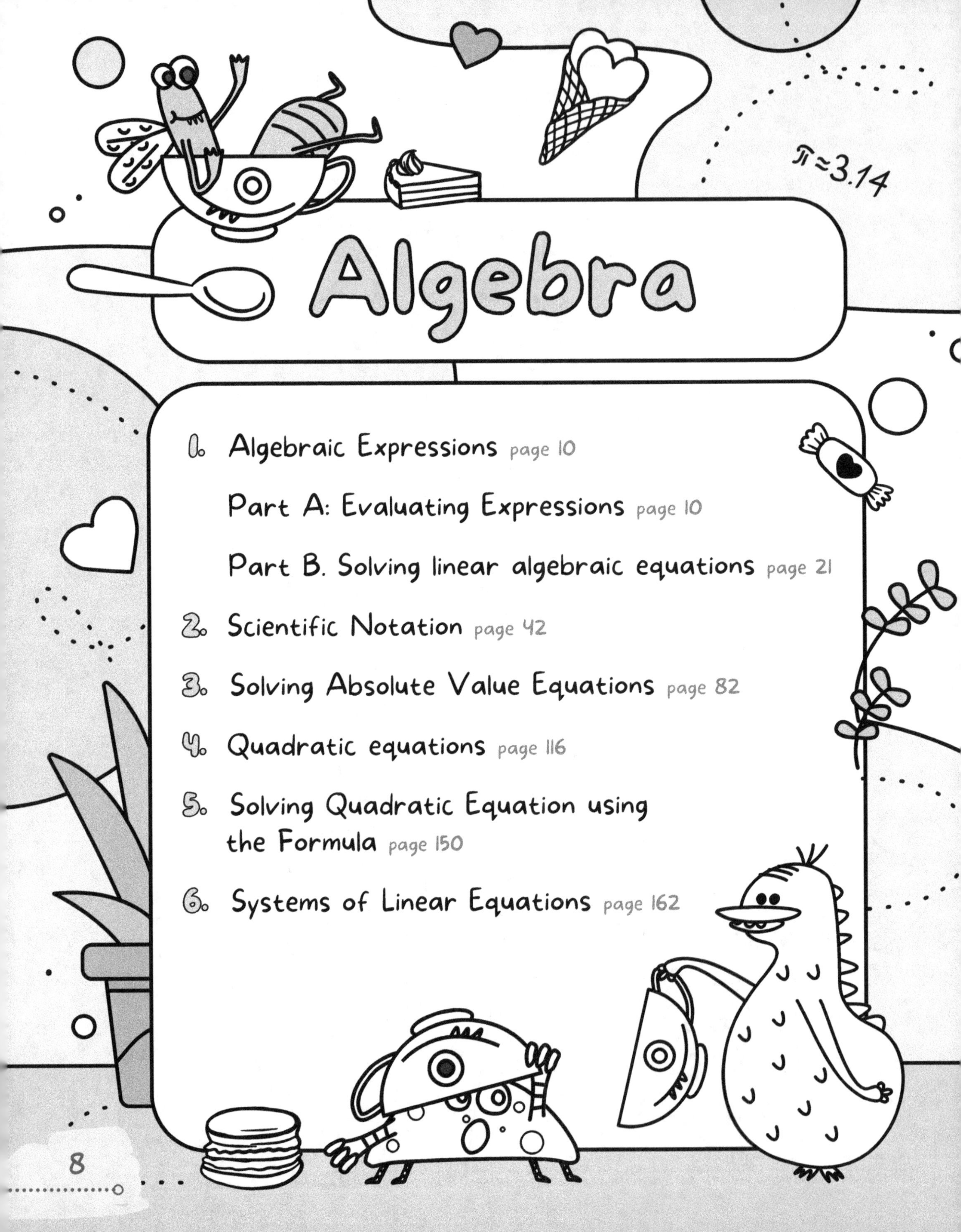

Algebra

c^2

a^2+b^2

$(x+y)^2=$

$k<0$

$\sqrt{2}$

$\dfrac{x}{x+2}-\dfrac{8}{x+6}=$

$\dfrac{\sqrt{3}}{2}$

Part A: Evaluating Expressions

An **algebraic expression** is a mathematical phrase that can contain **numbers, variables, and operators**. The most basic algebraic expressions are just a single variable, such as "x" or "y." More complex expressions can contain multiple variables, constants, and mathematical operations such as addition, subtraction, multiplication, and division.

For example, **"2x + 3"** is an algebraic expression. It contains the variable "x," a constant (the number 2), and the addition operator (+). The value of this expression will change depending on the value of the variable "x." If "x" is equal to **5**, then the expression equals $(2 \times 5) + 3 = 13$.

Another example of an algebraic expression is "3y - 4x." It contains two variables, "y" and "x," a constant (the number 3), and the subtraction operator (-). The value of this expression will also change depending on the values of the variables "x" and "y." If "x" is equal to **2** and "y" is equal to **4**, then the expression equals $3(4) - (4)2 = 12 - 8 = 4$.

Algebraic expressions can also include more advanced mathematical operations such as exponents and roots. For example, the expression **"x² + 5x + 6"** is an algebraic expression that contains a variable "x," two constants (**5 and 6**), and two operators (^ and +). The value of this expression will change depending on the value of "x." If "x" is equal to **2**, then the expression equals $2^2 + 5 \times 2 + 6 = 4 + 10 + 6 = 20$.

Algebraic expressions can also be combined using algebraic properties such as the distributive property and the commutative property. The distributive property allows us to multiply a single term by a sum or difference of multiple terms. For example, we can use the distributive property to simplify the expression **"3(x + 2) = 3x + 6"**. Similarly, the commutative property allows us to rearrange the order of the terms in an expression without changing its value. For example, we can use the commutative property to simplify the expression "3x + 4y = 4y + 3x".

Algebraic expressions are used in a wide variety of mathematical and scientific applications. In Algebra 1, they are used to represent mathematical relationships and equations, and to solve problems involving variables. This is the first topic covered in any Algebra 1 course.

Here are three guided practice examples for evaluating algebraic expressions:

Guided Practice Question #1:

Evaluate the expression **$2x + 3$** when **$x = 5$**.

Answer: $2(5) + 3 = 10 + 3 = 13$.

Explanation: To evaluate this expression, we substitute the value of x (5) into the expression and simplify. First, we multiply 2 by 5 to get 10. Then we add 3 to 10 to get the final answer of 13.

Guided Practice Question #2:

Evaluate the expression **$3y - 4x$** when **$x = 2$** and **$y = 4$**.

Answer: $3(4) - 4(2) = 12 - 8 = 4$.

Explanation: To evaluate this expression, we substitute the values of x and y (2 and 4) into the expression and simplify. First, we multiply 3 by 4 to get 12. Then we multiply 4 by 2 to get 8. Next, we subtract 8 from 12 to get the final answer of 4.

Guided Practice Question #3:

Evaluate the expression **$x^2 + 5x + 6$** when **$x = 2$**.

Answer: $2^2 + 5(2) + 6 = 4 + 10 + 6 = 20$.

Explanation: To evaluate this expression, we substitute the value of x into the expression and simplify. First, we square 2 to get 4. Next, we multiply 5 by 2 to get 10. Then we add 4, 10, and 6 to get the final answer of 20.

Please complete the following practice questions related to evaluating expressions.

Evaluate the expression using the values given

1. $z - (y + z)$; use $y = 7$, and $z = 7$

2. $(x + z)^2$; use $x = 8$, and $z = -6$

3. $-10m + p$; use $m = 7$, and $p = 9$

4. $z + y - 6$; use $y = -4$, and $z = -4$

5. $(-1) - (q + p)$; use $p = 6$, and $q = 9$

6. $y - 9x$; use $x = -3$, and $y = -1$

7. $y + x - x$; use $x = -6$, and $y = -3$

8. $x + \dfrac{z}{5}$; use $x = -1$, and $z = -5$

9. $p + q + q$; use $p = 1$, and $q = 10$

10. $a^2 - c$; use $a = -5$, and $c = 10$

11. $y \times \dfrac{x}{3}$; use $x = -3$, and $y = 6$

16. $a - b^2$; use $a = 6$, and $b = 8$

12. $c(c + b)$; use $b = 1$, and $c = 7$

17. $n + \dfrac{p}{6}$; use $n = 9$, and $p = -6$

13. $x(x - z)$; use $x = -6$, and $z = 9$

18. $p^3 - q$; use $p = 3$, and $q = -6$

14. $\dfrac{zx}{3}$; use $y = -2$, and $z = -4$

19. $q - \dfrac{p}{5}$; use $p = 5$, and $q = -3$

15. $k \times \dfrac{h}{2}$; use $h = -10$, and $k = -1$

20. $a - a - c$; use $a = -1$, and $c = 7$

21. $c + b + 5$; use $b = -1$, and $c = 10$

22. $b - a + 5$; use $a = -2$, and $b = -10$

23. $y - y - x$; use $x = -6$, and $y = -9$

24. $m + p - 2$; use $m = 8$, and $p = -8$

25. $q - (p - p)$; use $p = 6$, and $q = -6$

26. $m - \dfrac{q}{4}$; use $m = 3$, and $q = 8$

27. $p + 9 - m$; use $m = -4$, and $p = -4$

28. $p - (r + q)$; use $p = 1$, $q = -5$, and $r = -8$

29. $(x - z)^2$; use $x = 6$, and $z = -4$

30. $(p - q)^2$; use $p = 2$, and $q = 5$

31. $(-2) - (k - j)$; use $j = -4$, and $k = -8$

36. $pm - p$; use $m = -7$, and $p = 4$

32. zxy; use $x = -4$, $y = -5$, and $z = 4$

37. $m - (m + p) - m$; use $m = 2$, and $p = -4$

33. $z + 6x$; use $x = -4$, and $z = -6$

38. $p^2(q - 7)$; use $p = -3$, and $q = -4$

34. $p - (1 - m)$; use $m = -5$, and $p = 8$

39. $z - y^2 - y$; use $y = 5$, and $z = 4$

35. $x + y + z$; use $x = 4$, $y = -4$, and $z = -7$

40. $y - (x^2 - x)$; use $x = -8$, and $y = -9$

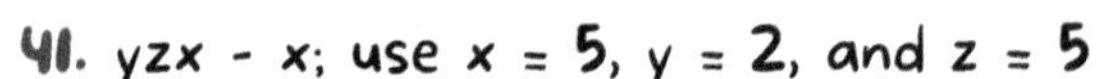

41. $yzx - x$; use $x = 5$, $y = 2$, and $z = 5$

46. $y\left(z - \dfrac{y}{3}\right)$; use $y = 3$, and $z = 4$

42. $x^2 + y - y$; use $x = -1$, and $y = -6$

47. $10 + \dfrac{rp}{4}$; use $p = -7$, and $r = -4$

43. $z^2 - (x - z)$; use $x = 8$, and $z = 4$

48. $h + 10 + \dfrac{j}{2}$; use $h = 8$, and $j = 2$

44. $q((-2) - qp)$; use $p = -1$, and $q = 8$

49. $-3x^2y$; use $x = 2$, and $y = -1$

45. $y((-6) + x) - y$; use $x = -10$, and $y = -5$

50. $ca \times \dfrac{b}{5}$; use $a = -3$, $b = -5$, and $c = 5$

51. $\dfrac{y(x-9)}{6}$; use $x = 3$, and $y = 9$

56. $q + p^2 - r$; use $p = -8$, $q = 6$, and $r = -10$

52. $\dfrac{b}{4} \times a^2$; use $a = 6$, and $b = 8$

57. $j + k - 4j$; use $j = 8$, and $k = -5$

53. $z \times \dfrac{y+y}{2}$; use $y = -7$, and $z = 4$

58. $(-8) - (y + y + x)$; use $x = 10$, and $y = 10$

54. $z \times \dfrac{xy}{3}$; use $x = 9$, $y = -3$, and $z = 9$

59. $-8p + m - m$; use $m = -1$, and $p = 4$

55. $qp \times \dfrac{m}{4}$; use $m = -4$, $p = -1$, and $q = 6$

60. $y - 2x^2$; use $x = 4$, and $y = 8$

61. $(-9) + b + a + c$; use $a = 4$, $b = 1$, and $c = 6$

62. $k(1 + j + h)$; use $h = 5$, $j = 4$, and $k = -1$

63. $p + 4 - (r - q)$; use $p = -8$, $q = 3$, and $r = 7$

64. $z + x - xy$; use $x = -2$, $y = 7$, and $z = -8$

65. $z - (x + y)^2$; use $x = -6$, $y = 9$, and $z = 7$

66. hjj^2; use $h = -1$, and $j = -4$

67. $x(x + y + y)$; use $x = 7$, and $y = -6$

68. $q(2 - m^2)$; use $m = 3$, and $q = -3$

69. $q - p + 8 + p$; use $p = 5$, and $q = -2$

70. $q + p + p$; use $p = -5$, and $q = -7$

71. $x + y + y + 4$; use $x = 9$, and $y = -4$

72. $m - 9 + p - 2$; use $m = -5$, and $p = 5$

73. $q(q + q) - r$; use $q = 4$, and $r = -10$

74. $x + 10y - z$; use $x = -5$, $y = 6$, and $z = -2$

75. $y(2 - (z - z))$; use $y = 2$, and $z = -2$

76. $q + m^3 + q$; use $m = -2$, and $q = 8$

77. $z + z + y^2$; use $y = -7$, and $z = 5$

78. $x + 10 + \dfrac{m}{4}$; use $x = 6$, and $z = 4$

79. $x(z - 8 - y)$; use $x = -1$, $y = -10$, and $z = -7$

80. $x + yz + z$; use $x = 6$, $y = 3$, and $z = -2$

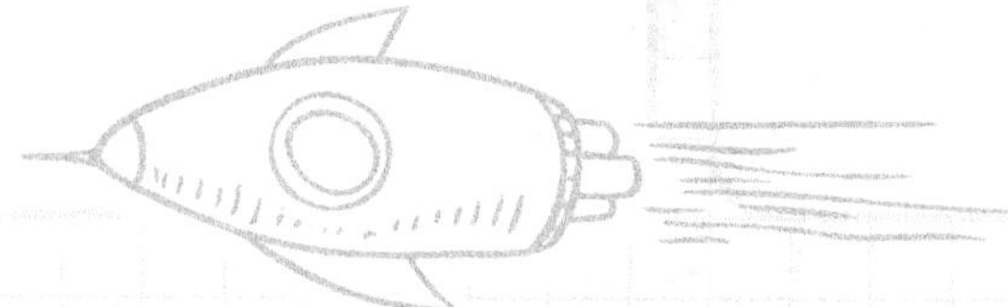

81. n - 7(m - n); use m = -5, and n = 7

86. x(z + z) + y; use x = 5, y = 3, and z = 3

82. $y \times \dfrac{z}{4} + 7$; use y = -8, and z = 8

87. n(p + n) - p; use n = -10, and p = 10

83. $\dfrac{x}{6} - (x - z)$; use x = -6, and z = -3

88. z - (z - xz); use x = -8, and z = -7

84. p(n - (9 - 10)); use n = 8, and p = 9

89. $\dfrac{y^2}{4} - z$; use y = -10, and z = 2

85. (-7) - (c² + b); use b = 1, and c = 3

90. $\dfrac{9}{3}(y - z)$; use y = 9, and z = 3

Part B. Solving linear algebraic equations

Solving one-step algebraic equations is the process of isolating the variable on one side of the equation by using inverse operations. An algebraic equation is an equation that contains one or more variables, such as x or y. The goal of solving an equation is to find the value of the variable that makes the equation true.

There are four basic operations that can be used to solve one-step algebraic equations: addition, subtraction, multiplication, and division. To solve an equation, we must use the inverse operation of the operation used to create the equation.

For example, if we are given the equation $2x = 6$, we can solve for x by dividing both sides of the equation by 2. This is the inverse operation of multiplication, and it allows us to isolate the variable on one side of the equation.

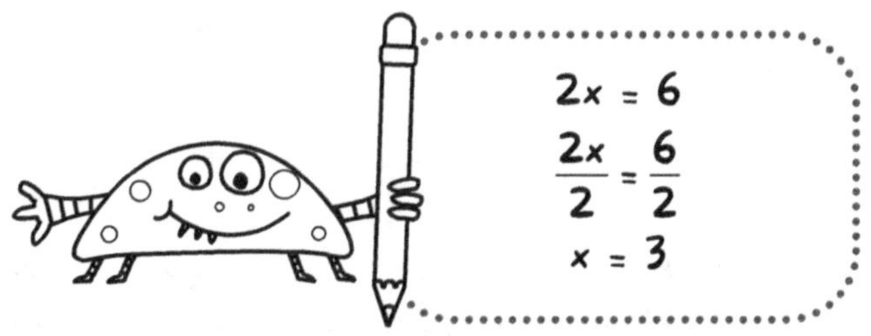

$$2x = 6$$
$$\frac{2x}{2} = \frac{6}{2}$$
$$x = 3$$

In this case, $x = 3$ is the solution to the equation.

Another example is if we have the equation $4x - 6 = 2$, we can solve for x by adding 6 to both sides of the equation and then dividing by 4.

$$4x - 6 = 2$$
$$4x - 6 + 6 = 2 + 6$$
$$4x = 8$$
$$\frac{4x}{4} = \frac{8}{4}$$
$$x = 2$$

In this case, $x = 2$ is the solution to the equation.

It's important to note that when solving algebraic equations, it's important to apply the order of operations (PEMDAS) which is Parentheses, Exponents, Multiplication and Division from left to right, Addition and Subtraction from left to right.

Finally, when solving one-step equations, it's also important to check your solution. To check your solution, you should substitute the value you found for the variable back into the original equation and see if it makes the equation true.

For example, to check the solution of $x = 3$ for the equation $2x = 6$, we substitute 3 in place of x:

$$2(3) = 6$$
$$6 = 6$$

which is true, so $x = 3$ is the correct solution.

Let's take a look at a few guided practice problems for solving one-step algebraic problems before you practice on your own.

Guided Practice Question #1:

$3x + 2 = 8$

Explanation: To solve for x, we need to isolate it on one side of the equation. We can do this by subtracting **2** from both sides. This gives us: $3x = 6$. Next, we divide both sides by **3**, which gives us $x = 2$.

Guided Practice Question #2:

$5y - 3 = 2y + 8$

Explanation: To solve for y, we need to isolate it on one side of the equation. We can do this by adding **3** to both sides, which gives us $5y = 2y + 11$. Next, we subtract $2y$ from both sides, which gives us $3y = 11$. Finally, we divide both sides by **3**, which gives us $y = 11/3$

Guided Practice Question #3:

$2z - 4 = 8 + z$

Explanation: To solve for z, we need to isolate it on one side of the equation. We can do this by subtracting z from both sides, which gives us $z - 4 = 8$. Next, we add **4** to both sides, which gives us $z = 12$.

Guided Practice Question #4:

$$-3 = \frac{n}{7}$$

Explanation: To solve for n, we need to isolate it on one side of the equation. We can do this by multiplying both sides by 7, which gives us -3(7) = n. Then we simplify the left side(-3 × 7) to get -21 = n.

Guided Practice Question #5:

$$7x + 2 + 6 = -7 + 2x + 8x$$

Explanation: To solve this equation for simplifying the like terms on both sides of the equation. On the left side, we can simplify it to "7x + 8" by adding 2 and 6. On the right side, we can simplify it to "-7 + 10x" by adding 2x + 8x.

We are left with the equation **7x + 8 = -7 + 10x**

Now, the goal is to isolate x on one side of the equation. You can do this in different ways. Subtract 7x on both sides so we are left with **8 = -7 + 3x**.

We need to get the "-7" to the left side, so we can do the inverse operation which is to add +7 to both sides. We are left with **15 = 3x**.

Finally, to isolate x, we divide both sides by 3 to get 5 = x.

The **answer** is **x = 5**.

Please complete the following practice questions related to solving algebraic equations.

Solve the equation

1. $p - 10 - 2p = 18 - 5p$

2. $18 - 9n = -2 - 7n - 6n$

3. $2 + 8n + n = -6 + 7n$

4. $4x + 20 = x + 2$

5. $3 + 6r = 6r - 3r$

6. $-1 - n + 6 = 7n + 2 + 4n - 9$

7. $4 + 5a = 4 + 10a$

8. $4 - 10x = -9x + 1$

9. $n - 1 = -9 - 8n + 10n$

10. $-10k + 10 = -2k + 2k$

11. $-10n - n = -15 - 6n$

16. $-9 + 9n = 10n - 3$

12. $9x + 3 = 17 + 7x$

17. $4x + 20 = 2x + 8$

13. $2v - 3 = 5 + 4v$

18. $8 + r = -18 + 9 + 4r - 10$

14. $n - 3 = 5 + 2n$

19. $x - 7x = 18 - 9x$

15. $-4 + 6x = 9x - 13$

20. $-8 + 4k + 9 - 5 = -5k - 9 - 4$

21. $-9a + 3a + 12 = -6a + 3a$

22. $-6x + 10 = -17 - 3x$

23. $-7k + 5 = -5k - 7$

24. $3m + 11 = -2m - 4$

25. $10k + 3 + 7k - 15 = 10k + 10k$

26. $3m + 1 = -9 + 4m$

27. $2x + 11 = x + 3$

28. $1 + 5x = -2x + 15$

29. $-8 + 8v = v - 1$

30. $10v + 1 + 10 = v - 7 - 5v + 4$

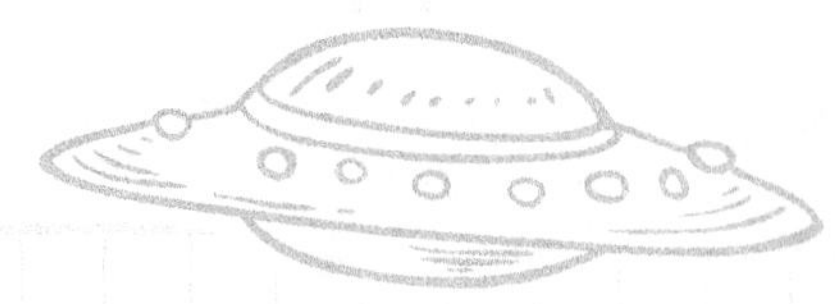

31. $-7 + 9x - 2x = -2 + 8x$

36. $20 - 6n = -4n + 4$

32. $-10 - 5v = 6v - 10$

37. $4x + 15 = 5x + 5$

33. $18 - 5r = 10 - 6r$

38. $11 - 2n = 3 + 2n + 4$

34. $-5 - 3m + 6m = m + m$

39. $16 + 3k = k + 4$

35. $-18 + x + 1 - 4 = 7 + 5x$

40. $-9 - 4m = 18 - m$

41. $-20 - 4x = 1 - 7x$

42. $-2x - 7 = -6x + 7 + 6x$

43. $13 + 5x + 4x = 8x + 7 + 2x$

44. $-10 + k = -6k - 3k$

45. $n - 6 = n - 9 + 4n + 19$

46. $14 + 9b = 2b + 9b$

47. $8 - 5p - 5 - 7 = 1 - 10p$

48. $7n + 7 = 1 + 8n$

49. $x - 2 + 6x = -2 + 2x$

50. $1 + 9x = 5 + 5x + 2x$

51. $-3v + 7 = -3 - 5v$

56. $6 + 2n - 4n = 7n - 10n$

52. $-8 - 5n - 8n = -8n - 7n$

57. $-11 + 4b = b + 7$

53. $-5 + 4v + 4 + 9 = v - 1$

58. $-4x + 9 = -8 + x + 7 - 4x$

54. $p + 7 - 3p = -3p$

59. $-8x + 8 = -5x - 7$

55. $7x + 2 = 2 + 5x$

60. $10r - 3 = 6r + 7r$

61. -8b = 4b - 2b

62. 10 + 3x = -15 + 8x

63. 3 - 3v = 11 - 6v + 1 + 2v

64. 9n - 10n = -3n + 16

65. -8n + 6n = n - 3 - 6n - 12

66. 1 + 6n = -8 - 5n + 10n

67. 6x - 1 = 9x + 11

68. -10 - 5x = 11 - 9x - 3x

69. 1 + 8k + 8k = 11 + 6k

70. 9 - 3n = 7 - 2n

71. $-7r + 6r + 10 = r - 10$

72. $-8b + 9 = -10b + 15$

73. $-12 + 3v = v - 2$

74. $7 + 5n = 13 + 6n$

75. $r + 2 - 5r = 6 - 8r$

76. $x + 8 = 15 + 8x - 8x$

77. $17 + 2n = n + 9$

78. $-8n - 8n = 20 - 4n - 10n$

79. $4x - 6 = x - 12$

80. $-8 + k = 1 + 2k$

81. $16 + 9b = 6b + 4$

86. $3n + 10 - 6 = 14 + 2n$

82. $-18 - 6n = -8n + 4n$

87. $-5 + 3v = 4v - 10$

83. $7n - 15 = 1 + 9n$

88. $-2b + 2 = 17 - b - 8 - 3$

84. $-8x - 9x = 15 + 1 - 6x - 7x$

89. $-10 - 2p = 4p - 4p$

85. $1 + 9x = 6x + 7$

90. $6x - x = -2 + 9x - 3x$

91. $13 = n + 5$

92. $13 = p - 3$

93. $m + 23 = 7$

94. $-3 = 1 + x$

95. $14 = n - (-17)$

96. $21 = -8 - r$

97. $32 = b + 21$

98. $-3 + a = -5$

99. $-8 = -28 - n$

100. $k + (-22) = -7$

101. $\dfrac{a}{18} = 29$

106. $n - (-26) = 30$

102. $28 + p = 32$

107. $m + 21 = 10$

103. $115 = 23x$

108. $-26 + b = -15$

104. $-459 = 27x$

109. $12 = 15 + x$

105. $\dfrac{10}{9} = \dfrac{x}{9}$

110. $-25 = -25v$

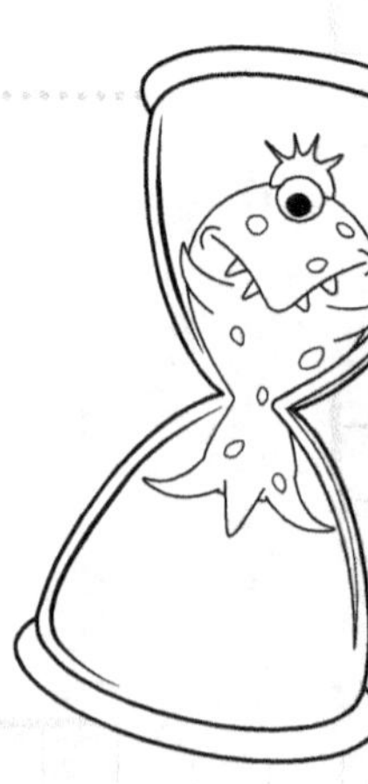

111. $20x = -60$

116. $-22 = p + 5$

112. $-22 - x = -35$

117. $-5 = 1 - x$

113. $-280 = -14n$

118. $21 = \dfrac{k}{11}$

114. $105 = -21a$

119. $5a = -145$

115. $n + 30 = 12$

120. $\dfrac{x}{18} = -11$

121. $-18 + n = 1$

122. $-29 = \dfrac{m}{21}$

123. $36 = m - (-10)$

124. $8 = x - 14$

125. $\dfrac{b}{8} = -25$

126. $29 + k = 49$

127. $-8 = \dfrac{n}{25}$

128. $a + (-2) = -12$

129. $-19 = -8 + n$

130. $6 = \dfrac{k}{14}$

131. $-4 = x - 8$

136. $-2 = -28 - x$

132. $a + 6 = 10$

137. $\frac{n}{13} = 20$

133. $-126 = -14x$

138. $-12 = 9 - r$

134. $14k = -406$

139. $29 - n = 4$

135. $\frac{k}{14} = -13$

140. $40 = 20 + a$

141. $-26 = \dfrac{x}{29}$

142. $v + 29 = 28$

143. $-12b = -48$

144. $\dfrac{k}{6} = 3$

145. $\dfrac{x}{16} = -\dfrac{27}{16}$

146. $-29 = n + (-10)$

147. $6n = -66$

148. $r - 9 = -15$

149. $65 = 5m$

150. $-13 = \dfrac{r}{3}$

151. $\dfrac{n}{2} = -4$

152. $\dfrac{m}{15} = -21$

153. $-2 = -19 - x$

154. $34 = 2n$

155. $n - 8 = -10$

156. $-3 = v - (-24)$

157. $\dfrac{a}{14} = 13$

158. $\dfrac{x}{10} = -5$

159. $-120 = -5x$

160. $-23 - r = -37$

161. $n - 22 = -41$

162. $-17 = \dfrac{x}{17}$

163. $a + (-18) = -45$

164. $-15 = \dfrac{a}{22}$

165. $-616 = 22n$

166. $\dfrac{p}{17} = -24$

167. $r + (-30) = -13$

168. $\dfrac{r}{23} = -9$

169. $-25 = x + (-17)$

170. $16k = -304$

171. $-216 = -18r$

172. $32 = m + 5$

173. $19 = \dfrac{p}{5}$

174. $k + 13 = 24$

175. $-116 = 4x$

176. $-36 = b - 12$

177. $-20 = \dfrac{k}{10}$

178. $0 = -4 + b$

179. $18b = 486$

180. $23 = \dfrac{a}{27}$

Scientific notation is a way of expressing numbers that are either very large or very small in a more convenient and compact form. For Algebra I, you will need to be very comfortable working with simplifying expressions in scientific notation.

In scientific notation, a number is written as a **mantissa** (a number between 1 and 10) multiplied by a power of 10. The power of 10 represents the number of zeroes in the original number. For example, the number 0.000001 (1 millionth) can be written in scientific notation as 1×10^{-6}. The number 100,000,000 can be written as 1×10^8.

The mantissa is always a number between 1 and 10 and the exponent is always an integer. This allows for easy comparison of numbers with very different magnitudes, such as the distance between the Earth and the Sun, or the size of a molecule compared to the size of an atom.

Here's a few examples of numbers that are written in scientific notation:

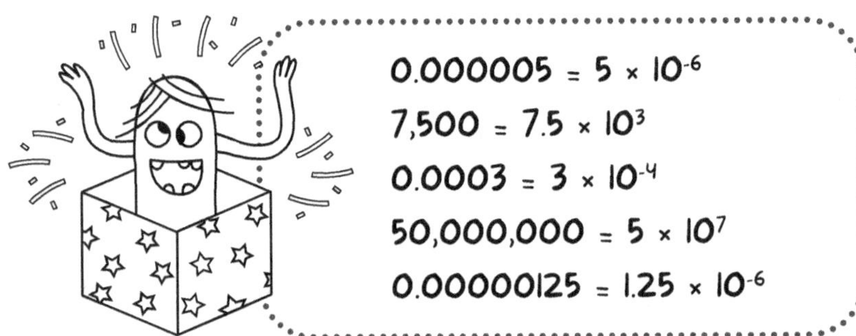

$$0.000005 = 5 \times 10^{-6}$$
$$7{,}500 = 7.5 \times 10^3$$
$$0.0003 = 3 \times 10^{-4}$$
$$50{,}000{,}000 = 5 \times 10^7$$
$$0.00000125 = 1.25 \times 10^{-6}$$

It is important to note that when performing mathematical operations with numbers in scientific notation, the exponent must be the same for both numbers before the operation can take place. For example, to add or subtract two numbers, their exponents must be the same. To multiply or divide two numbers, you simply add or subtract the exponents, respectively.

For example:

- $(5 \times 10^8) + (2 \times 10^8) = (5 + 2) \times 10^8 = 7 \times 10^8$
- $(5 \times 10^8) \times (2 \times 10^4) = (5 \times 2) \times (10^8 \times 10^4) = 10 \times 10^{12} = 10 \times 10^{12}$

Here are a few rules and examples of how to simplify expressions in scientific notation:

- **Adding or subtracting two numbers:** If the exponents are the same, you can add or subtract the mantissas and keep the exponent the same.

  For example, $(5 \times 10^8) + (2 \times 10^8) = (5 + 2) \times 10^8 = 7 \times 10^8$.

- **Multiplying two numbers:** To multiply two numbers in scientific notation, you multiply the mantissas and add the exponents.
  For example, $(5 \times 10^8) \times (2 \times 10^4) = (5 \times 2) \times (10^8 \times 10^4) = 10 \times 10^{12}$.

- **Dividing two numbers:** To divide two numbers in scientific notation, you divide the mantissas and subtract the exponents. For example, $\dfrac{5 \times 10^8}{2 \times 10^7} = \dfrac{5}{2} \times \dfrac{10^8}{10^4} = 2.5 \times 10^4$.

- **Raising a number to a power:** To raise a number in scientific notation to a power, you raise the mantissa to that power and multiply the exponent by the power.
  For example, $(3 \times 10^4)^2 = (3^2) \times (10^4)^2 = 9 \times 10^8$

Let's take a look at a few guided practice problems for simplifying and writing in scientific notation.

Guided Practice Question #1:

$(3.13 \times 10^5) (4 \times 10^4)$

Explanation: Notice that we are multiplying two numbers, so we know we need to multiply the mantissas and add the exponents. First, we will multiply 3.13×4 which gives us 12.52.

Next, we add the exponents $(5 + 4) = 9$. So we have 12.52×10^9. Please note: this is not the right answer. Although this is correct, it is not written in the proper scientific notation. There must be a decimal point immediately after the first number, so instead of 12.52 we need to get the number to 1.252. To do this, it's simple! To get from 1.252 to 12.52 we need to multiply by 10, meaning we are just adding 1 to the exponent.

So instead of $12.52 \times 10^{\wedge}9$ we will re-write this to 1.252×10^{10}, which is the answer.

Guided Practice Question #2:

$(6.5 \times 10^{-4}) (2 \times 10^6)$

Explanation: Similar to the question above, we are multiplying two numbers, so we need to follow the rule where we multiply the mantissa and add the exponents.

$6.5 \times 2 = 13$ and the exponents added are $-4 + 6$ to get 2.

We can write this as 13×10^2, however, note this is not written in scientific notation. The 13 must be written as 1.3 and so we will add 1 to the exponent, making the correct answer 1.3×10^3.

Guided Practice Question #3:

$$\frac{3.33 \times 10^4}{5.1 \times 10^{-6}}$$

Explanation: Notice that we are dividing two numbers, so we know we need to divide the mantissas and subtract the exponents. For these questions, feel free to use a calculator since you will be dividing numbers with decimals.

Step 1: Divide the mantissas $\frac{3.33}{5.1} = 0.6529$

Step 2: Subtract exponents $4 - (-6) = 10$

We currently have 0.6529×10^{10}. However, this is not written in the proper scientific notation. The mantissa cannot be 0. The first number must be **6** followed by a decimal point, so we are multiplying the mantissa by 10. Since we are doing this, we need to subtract the exponent by 1, making it 6.529×10^9.

Guided Practice Question #4:

$$(2.3 \times 10^5)^3$$

Explanation: We are raising to a power, so we need to follow the rule that we discussed above for raising a number to a power. To raise a number in scientific notation to a power, you raise the mantissa to that power and multiply the exponent by the power.

Step 1: $2.3^3 = 12.167$

Step 2: The exponent is 5 and we are raising to the power of 3. We need to multiply these two numbers. $5 \times 3 = 15$.

We have 12.167×10^{15}, however, this is **not** written in the proper scientific notation. We need to rewrite it to 1.2167×10^{16}.

*Tip: In the case of 1.2167, most textbooks and exams will round up to the thousandth place. So we can just write this as 1.217×10^{16}.

Guided Practice Question #5:

$$\frac{1.98 \times 10^3}{2 \times 10^{-2}}$$

Explanation: Similar to the question above, we are dividing two numbers, so we need to follow the rule where we divide the mantissa and subtract the exponents. For these questions, feel free to use a calculator since you will be dividing numbers with decimals.

Step 1: Divide the mantissas $\frac{1.98}{2} = 0.99$

Step 2: Subtract exponents $3 - (-2) = 5$

We currently have 0.99×10^5. However, this is not written in the proper scientific notation. The mantissa cannot be 0. The first number must be 9 followed by a decimal point, so we are multiplying the mantissa by 10. Since we are doing this, we need to subtract the exponent by 1, making it 9.9×10^4.

Guided Practice Question #6:

$$(6 \times 10^{-2})^4$$

Explanation: We are raising to a power, so we need to follow the rule that we discussed above for raising a number to a power. To raise a number in scientific notation to a power, you raise the mantissa to that power and multiply the exponent by the power.

Step 1: $6^4 = 1296$

Step 2: The exponent is -2 and we are raising to the power of 4. We need to multiply these two numbers. $-2 \times 4 = -8$.

We have 1296×10^{-8} however, this is **not** written in the proper scientific notation. We need to rewrite it to 1.296. You will notice that going from 1296 to 1.296 means we moved the decimal place back 3 times, so to keep the same value it is 1.296×10^3.

We have 10^3 and 10^{-8}, which the rule state when you have the same base, you just add the exponents. In this case, we have $3 + (-8) = -5$.

Therefore, the answer is 1.296×10^{-5}.

Please complete the following questions related to simplifying numbers dealing with scientific notation.

Simplify. Write each answer in scientific notation

1. $(6.1 \times 10^{-3})^2$

2. $(9 \times 10^3)^4$

3. $(3 \times 10^{-1})(8.5 \times 10^5)$

4. $\dfrac{1.5 \times 10^5}{5.35 \times 10^{-6}}$

5. $(1.76 \times 10^1)^6$

6. $(4.5 \times 10^{-3})^3$

7. $(4.1 \times 10^{-2})(4.1 \times 10^{-6})$

8. $(3.52 \times 10^3)^3$

9. $\dfrac{2.4 \times 10^6}{8 \times 10^3}$

10. $(9.07 \times 10^0)(8 \times 10^3)$

11. $(5 \times 10^2)^{-2}$

16. $\dfrac{3.79 \times 10^1}{1.3 \times 10^{-3}}$

12. $(3 \times 10^5)(1.54 \times 10^{-4})$

17. $(5 \times 10^4)(2.01 \times 10^1)$

13. $(6.7 \times 10^2)(8 \times 10^{-2})$

18. $(7.4 \times 10^{-2})^2$

14. $\dfrac{9.18 \times 10^5}{7.8 \times 10^0}$

19. $(8.69 \times 10^{-2})^6$

15. $\dfrac{8 \times 10^0}{6.4 \times 10^{-1}}$

20. $(7.4 \times 10^2)(6.2 \times 10^{-4})$

21. $\dfrac{9.1 \times 10^6}{4 \times 10^{-2}}$

22. $(7.2 \times 10^1)(5.1 \times 10^3)$

23. $(5.8 \times 10^5)(9 \times 10^4)$

24. $\dfrac{7.72 \times 10^{-1}}{3.4 \times 10^0}$

25. $\dfrac{3.1 \times 10^{-4}}{7 \times 10^{-3}}$

26. $(9 \times 10^1)(4.7 \times 10^6)$

27. $\dfrac{3.1 \times 10^4}{2.8 \times 10^{-5}}$

28. $(8 \times 10^{-5})(9.9 \times 10^4)$

29. $\dfrac{5 \times 10^{-3}}{5.4 \times 10^{-5}}$

30. $\dfrac{8.4 \times 10^0}{9.19 \times 10^{-6}}$

31. $\dfrac{5.88 \times 10^{-4}}{8.5 \times 10^{-4}}$

36. $(3.4 \times 10^{-5})(9.75 \times 10^{-1})$

32. $\dfrac{2 \times 10^{3}}{2.7 \times 10^{0}}$

37. $(4.9 \times 10^{3})(6.3 \times 10^{1})$

33. $\dfrac{3.08 \times 10^{4}}{1.3 \times 10^{-1}}$

38. $(3 \times 10^{5})(6.31 \times 10^{0})$

34. $\dfrac{2 \times 10^{-4}}{2.9 \times 10^{-6}}$

39. $\dfrac{2.72 \times 10^{1}}{9 \times 10^{3}}$

35. $\dfrac{6 \times 10^{-1}}{4 \times 10^{4}}$

40. $(7.16 \times 10^{6})(1.3 \times 10^{-2})$

41. $(5.21 \times 10^5)(5 \times 10^0)$

46. $(6.6 \times 10^0)(4.59 \times 10^5)$

42. $(6 \times 10^{-3})^3$

47. $(2.89 \times 10^5)(4.4 \times 10^{-1})$

43. $\dfrac{7.9 \times 10^{-2}}{5.71 \times 10^3}$

48. $\dfrac{9 \times 10^{-4}}{1.75 \times 10^{-3}}$

44. $(3.6 \times 10^5)^3$

49. $(2.06 \times 10^{-3})^4$

45. $(8.6 \times 10^1)(9 \times 10^3)$

50. $\dfrac{3.3 \times 10^{-1}}{3.5 \times 10^{-5}}$

51. $\dfrac{7.9 \times 10^{1}}{5.16 \times 10^{2}}$

56. $(1.02 \times 10^{2})(5.81 \times 10^{-3})$

52. $(8.23 \times 10^{1})(5.4 \times 10^{-2})$

57. $(9.8 \times 10^{5})(4 \times 10^{-1})$

53. $(5 \times 10^{6})(5.04 \times 10^{1})$

58. $\dfrac{8 \times 10^{0}}{2.6 \times 10^{4}}$

54. $\dfrac{2.2 \times 10^{3}}{2.09 \times 10^{5}}$

59. $(5.1 \times 10^{-1})^{5}$

55. $(9.2 \times 10^{4})(9.48 \times 10^{2})$

60. $(9.48 \times 10^{2})(6 \times 10^{5})$

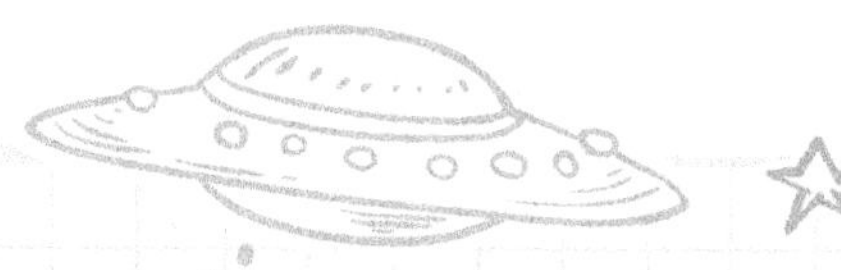

61. $\dfrac{1.06 \times 10^2}{1.3 \times 10^0}$

66. $\dfrac{3.6 \times 10^6}{2.45 \times 10^{-6}}$

62. $\dfrac{4.18 \times 10^6}{8.5 \times 10^{-2}}$

67. $(1.9 \times 10^{-3})(4.61 \times 10^0)$

63. $(5.8 \times 10^5)(6.94 \times 10^2)$

68. $(6.3 \times 10^{-4})(4 \times 10^{-6})$

64. $(5.32 \times 10^6)^2$

69. $\dfrac{3.2 \times 10^2}{2.04 \times 10^{-1}}$

65. $(2.1 \times 10^1)(4.43 \times 10^{-2})$

70. $(7.1 \times 10^6)^3$

71. $\dfrac{4.7 \times 10^{-3}}{4.69 \times 10^{-1}}$

76. $(3 \times 10^6)(6 \times 10^4)$

72. $(5 \times 10^4)^2$

77. $\dfrac{9.6 \times 10^{-3}}{4.3 \times 10^{-5}}$

73. $(9.3 \times 10^{-3})(2 \times 10^{-4})$

78. $\dfrac{4.14 \times 10^5}{8.4 \times 10^{-3}}$

74. $(1.11 \times 10^{-6})(8 \times 10^{-6})$

79. $\dfrac{7.15 \times 10^{-4}}{3.31 \times 10^2}$

75. $\dfrac{1.8 \times 10^1}{4.4 \times 10^{-5}}$

80. $(6.2 \times 10^{-2})^2$

81. $(2.8 \times 10^{-1})(2 \times 10^4)$

82. $\dfrac{4.72 \times 10^6}{3 \times 10^{-5}}$

83. $\dfrac{6.4 \times 10^{-6}}{3.41 \times 10^3}$

84. $\dfrac{2.8 \times 10^{-6}}{4.1 \times 10^{-5}}$

85. $\dfrac{9 \times 10^{-4}}{7.6 \times 10^{-1}}$

86. $(5.3 \times 10^5)(3.9 \times 10^{-3})$

87. $\dfrac{7.89 \times 10^6}{7 \times 10^{-1}}$

88. $(8.6 \times 10^{-3})(8.1 \times 10^4)$

89. $(3.3 \times 10^{-2})^6$

90. $(2.3 \times 10^{-1})^6$

91. $\dfrac{4 \times 10^5}{6 \times 10^{-1}}$

96. $(6 \times 10^{-1})^5$

92. $\dfrac{3.5 \times 10^0}{7.8 \times 10^2}$

97. $(2.58 \times 10^{-4})(8.2 \times 10^2)$

93. $(1.4 \times 10^{-6})(7 \times 10^{-4})$

98. $(8.09 \times 10^4)(5.3 \times 10^{-4})$

94. $\dfrac{2 \times 10^0}{2.7 \times 10^0}$

99. $\dfrac{7.63 \times 10^0}{4.3 \times 10^{-1}}$

95. $\dfrac{6.14 \times 10^3}{6.9 \times 10^{-5}}$

100. $\dfrac{1.82 \times 10^3}{5 \times 10^4}$

101. $(2.1 \times 10^3)^5$

106. $\dfrac{7.5 \times 10^6}{2.9 \times 10^{-5}}$

102. $\dfrac{9.3 \times 10^4}{6.74 \times 10^5}$

107. $(2 \times 10^{-1})(6.76 \times 10^{-4})$

103. $\dfrac{8.5 \times 10^4}{7.7 \times 10^{-3}}$

108. $(1.3 \times 10^{-6})(7.6 \times 10^{-4})$

104. $\dfrac{7.59 \times 10^{-2}}{6.2 \times 10^0}$

109. $(2.1 \times 10^2)(9.31 \times 10^1)$

105. $(8.98 \times 10^4)(7.89 \times 10^{-6})$

110. $(3.2 \times 10^0)^2$

111. $(2.98 \times 10^4)^3$

116. $\dfrac{6 \times 10^{-1}}{8 \times 10^5}$

112. $(4.03 \times 10^{-6})(4 \times 10^5)$

117. $\dfrac{8.1 \times 10^2}{2.2 \times 10^4}$

113. $(6.18 \times 10^3)(1.5 \times 10^{-4})$

118. $\dfrac{8.6 \times 10^{-5}}{9 \times 10^5}$

114. $(8.4 \times 10^3)(1.13 \times 10^{-6})$

119. $\dfrac{8.1 \times 10^6}{2.5 \times 10^0}$

115. $\dfrac{6.41 \times 10^4}{7.17 \times 10^2}$

120. $(6 \times 10^2)(6.7 \times 10^{-1})$

121. $\dfrac{4.3 \times 10^4}{7.05 \times 10^1}$

122. $\dfrac{3.4 \times 10^4}{4 \times 10^3}$

123. $(5.7 \times 10^1)(9 \times 10^{-2})$

124. $(1.47 \times 10^2)(5.5 \times 10^6)$

125. $\dfrac{8.04 \times 10^{-1}}{7.5 \times 10^{-1}}$

126. $(7 \times 10^{-4})(6.5 \times 10^{-1})$

127. $(6 \times 10^4)^3$

128. $(3.17 \times 10^{-2})(6.6 \times 10^6)$

129. $(9.05 \times 10^{-5})(7.25 \times 10^{-2})$

130. $(6.7 \times 10^5)(5.4 \times 10^{-2})$

131. $(8.8 \times 10^{-3})^2$

132. $\dfrac{7.7 \times 10^{-1}}{5.4 \times 10^{6}}$

133. $(2.53 \times 10^{1})^6$

134. $\dfrac{2.6 \times 10^{-5}}{9 \times 10^{-5}}$

135. $(8.2 \times 10^{-5})(1.3 \times 10^{-4})$

136. $(2.6 \times 10^{3})(2.6 \times 10^{1})$

137. $\dfrac{4 \times 10^{-4}}{1.43 \times 10^{5}}$

138. $(2.99 \times 10^{-3})(7.7 \times 10^{6})$

139. $(6.66 \times 10^{0})^2$

140. $(1.6 \times 10^{4})^2$

141. $(4 \times 10^{-5})(9.48 \times 10^{-4})$

142. $\dfrac{3.02 \times 10^6}{2.13 \times 10^{-5}}$

143. $\dfrac{6 \times 10^6}{9 \times 10^{-2}}$

144. $\dfrac{5.05 \times 10^{-6}}{7.16 \times 10^4}$

145. $(4.9 \times 10^3)(1.53 \times 10^6)$

146. $(3 \times 10^1)(6.4 \times 10^5)$

147. $(5.6 \times 10^4)(9.6 \times 10^{-1})$

148. $(5.93 \times 10^{-1})(2.6 \times 10^{-2})$

149. $(2.1 \times 10^{-4})(2.9 \times 10^{-2})$

150. $(2 \times 10^{-6})(1.2 \times 10^{-3})$

151. $\dfrac{3.3 \times 10^0}{3 \times 10^{-1}}$

152. $\dfrac{1.6 \times 10^{-1}}{3 \times 10^0}$

153. $(8.6 \times 10^3)(2 \times 10^0)$

154. $(2.8 \times 10^{-6})(6.5 \times 10^6)$

155. $\dfrac{3.3 \times 10^3}{2.8 \times 10^{-6}}$

156. $\dfrac{8.8 \times 10^{-1}}{9.5 \times 10^{-4}}$

157. $\dfrac{4 \times 10^5}{1.59 \times 10^6}$

158. $\dfrac{5.44 \times 10^3}{3 \times 10^{-6}}$

159. $\dfrac{3 \times 10^{-1}}{5.2 \times 10^{-6}}$

160. $(9.4 \times 10^{-4})(2.7 \times 10^0)$

161. $(5.7 \times 10^2)^3$

166. $(8.14 \times 10^{-2})^4$

162. $\dfrac{8 \times 10^{-2}}{9 \times 10^{-4}}$

167. $\dfrac{3.27 \times 10^{-3}}{3.4 \times 10^0}$

163. $(5.02 \times 10^{-6})(7.81 \times 10^4)$

168. $(1.6 \times 10^{-1})(6.9 \times 10^{-1})$

164. $(9 \times 10^{-2})(5.75 \times 10^5)$

169. $\dfrac{7.3 \times 10^3}{9 \times 10^{-5}}$

165. $\dfrac{5.9 \times 10^{-1}}{7.7 \times 10^{-1}}$

170. $\dfrac{5 \times 10^4}{6 \times 10^{-2}}$

171. $\dfrac{9.2 \times 10^6}{3 \times 10^3}$

176. $(9.3 \times 10^{-5})(3.2 \times 10^1)$

172. $\dfrac{4 \times 10^{-5}}{4.37 \times 10^{-4}}$

177. $(9.74 \times 10^6)(6.6 \times 10^{-5})$

173. $(9.68 \times 10^{-6})(7 \times 10^{-6})$

178. $(3 \times 10^1)(5.6 \times 10^{-4})$

174. $(6.1 \times 10^{-5})(1.97 \times 10^6)$

179. $\dfrac{9 \times 10^6}{7.3 \times 10^5}$

175. $\dfrac{2.05 \times 10^2}{2 \times 10^{-3}}$

180. $\dfrac{3 \times 10^3}{5 \times 10^1}$

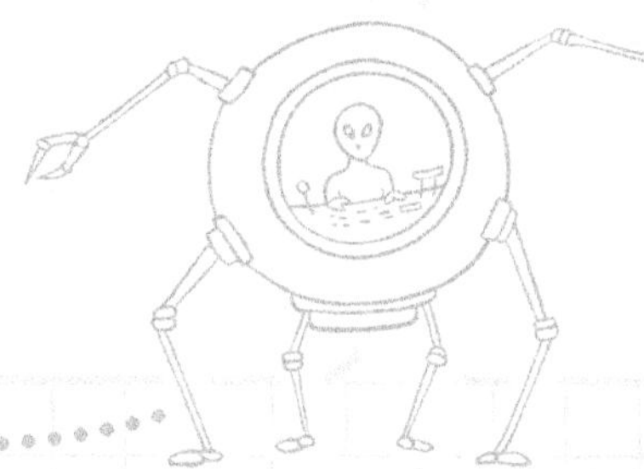

181. $(6.44 \times 10^4)(8.4 \times 10^{-6})$

182. $(1.4 \times 10^2)(3.87 \times 10^{-6})$

183. $\dfrac{9.37 \times 10^5}{5.5 \times 10^6}$

184. $\dfrac{9.5 \times 10^3}{8.1 \times 10^{-2}}$

185. $\dfrac{4 \times 10^{-6}}{1.65 \times 10^{-1}}$

186. $(6 \times 10^3)(6.7 \times 10^{-6})$

187. $(9 \times 10^{-4})^3$

188. $(7.8 \times 10^{-6})(4.7 \times 10^0)$

189. $\dfrac{6 \times 10^{-2}}{8.2 \times 10^{-1}}$

190. $\dfrac{8.93 \times 10^0}{5 \times 10^6}$

191. $\dfrac{2 \times 10^2}{5.33 \times 10^{-1}}$

196. $(8.2 \times 10^0)(2.2 \times 10^{-5})$

192. $(1.3 \times 10^{-2})(4.4 \times 10^{-1})$

197. $\dfrac{3.6 \times 10^1}{4 \times 10^{-5}}$

193. $\dfrac{5.76 \times 10^3}{3.7 \times 10^2}$

198. $(2.3 \times 10^{-2})(2.07 \times 10^{-5})$

194. $(6 \times 10^{-3})(3.25 \times 10^{-3})$

199. $\dfrac{3.8 \times 10^{-3}}{6.5 \times 10^1}$

195. $(7.7 \times 10^{-3})(9 \times 10^5)$

200. $(6.61 \times 10^5)(7.8 \times 10^{-1})$

201. $(7.9 \times 10^1)(4 \times 10^0)$

202. $\dfrac{3.2 \times 10^{-2}}{9.6 \times 10^6}$

203. $(5 \times 10^{-2})(6.9 \times 10^{-6})$

204. $\dfrac{4 \times 10^3}{2.97 \times 10^{-6}}$

205. $(9.3 \times 10^5)(6 \times 10^{-5})$

206. $\dfrac{9.6 \times 10^2}{7 \times 10^{-3}}$

207. $(4 \times 10^{-3})^4$

208. $(2.1 \times 10^1)(4.3 \times 10^3)$

209. $(8.8 \times 10^2)^2$

210. $(1.34 \times 10^4)^6$

211. $(7.5 \times 10^3)(2.4 \times 10^{-5})$

212. $(8 \times 10^{-6})(7 \times 10^0)$

213. $(2.8 \times 10^5)(4.27 \times 10^{-6})$

214. $(4.21 \times 10^{-2})(6.1 \times 10^{-5})$

215. $\dfrac{3 \times 10^3}{9.42 \times 10^2}$

216. $(3 \times 10^{-1})(5.62 \times 10^5)$

217. $\dfrac{3 \times 10^{-6}}{7.9 \times 10^6}$

218. $(3.67 \times 10^{-5})(8.4 \times 10^{-2})$

219. $\dfrac{5.1 \times 10^{-4}}{9.18 \times 10^3}$

220. $(3.6 \times 10^5)^2$

221. $\dfrac{6.39 \times 10^3}{9.6 \times 10^{-6}}$

226. $(9.6 \times 10^1)^{-2}$

222. $(5.4 \times 10^3)^3$

227. $(2.1 \times 10^{-3})(4.2 \times 10^0)$

223. $(2.5 \times 10^3)(1.1 \times 10^{-4})$

228. $(4.8 \times 10^3)(9 \times 10^5)$

224. $\dfrac{9.3 \times 10^5}{3.39 \times 10^{-6}}$

229. $(9 \times 10^5)^5$

225. $(8.1 \times 10^2)(6.15 \times 10^{-2})$

230. $(6 \times 10^1)(1.78 \times 10^{-4})$

231. $(9 \times 10^{-4})(5.2 \times 10^5)$

236. $\dfrac{9 \times 10^{-6}}{4 \times 10^4}$

232. $\dfrac{6.3 \times 10^{-2}}{2.7 \times 10^4}$

237. $(6.1 \times 10^6)(6 \times 10^5)$

233. $(9.67 \times 10^6)(8.6 \times 10^{-1})$

238. $(6 \times 10^2)^3$

234. $\dfrac{9.9 \times 10^6}{5 \times 10^2}$

239. $(4.27 \times 10^{-5})(5.2 \times 10^{-1})$

235. $\dfrac{8 \times 10^3}{8.61 \times 10^6}$

240. $(2 \times 10^{-6})(2.1 \times 10^0)$

241. $\dfrac{9.4 \times 10^{-6}}{5.71 \times 10^{-4}}$

246. $(4 \times 10^{-6})(5.37 \times 10^{2})$

242. $\dfrac{3.47 \times 10^{4}}{1.4 \times 10^{-1}}$

247. $\dfrac{2.1 \times 10^{1}}{3.5 \times 10^{3}}$

243. $(8.39 \times 10^{-4})(6.52 \times 10^{-5})$

248. $(5.01 \times 10^{-3})^{6}$

244. $\dfrac{9.6 \times 10^{6}}{9.7 \times 10^{3}}$

249. $(5 \times 10^{-5})^{6}$

245. $\dfrac{7.46 \times 10^{-5}}{8 \times 10^{5}}$

250. $\dfrac{7 \times 10^{3}}{9.3 \times 10^{-4}}$

251. $\dfrac{5.6 \times 10^{-3}}{9.4 \times 10^{5}}$

256. $\dfrac{4.2 \times 10^{-3}}{6.9 \times 10^{6}}$

252. $\dfrac{5 \times 10^{6}}{3.81 \times 10^{0}}$

257. $\dfrac{6.5 \times 10^{-6}}{3.33 \times 10^{5}}$

253. $\dfrac{8.5 \times 10^{1}}{9.44 \times 10^{-4}}$

258. $(9.82 \times 10^{-2})(8.7 \times 10^{-6})$

254. $(7.7 \times 10^{-3})(6.3 \times 10^{6})$

259. $\dfrac{8.97 \times 10^{0}}{8.6 \times 10^{-6}}$

255. $\dfrac{7 \times 10^{2}}{7.4 \times 10^{0}}$

260. $\dfrac{2 \times 10^{-1}}{5 \times 10^{5}}$

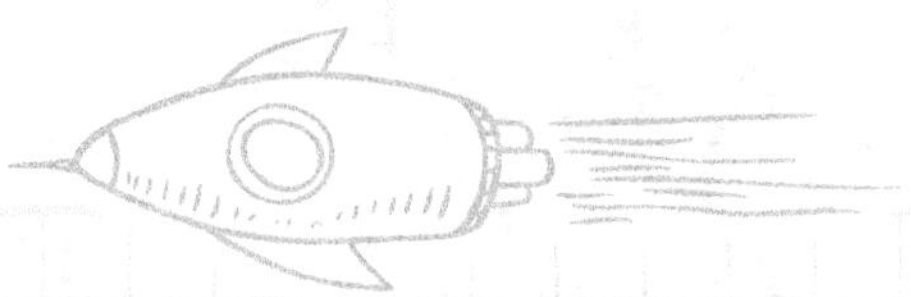

261. $\dfrac{4.2 \times 10^4}{9 \times 10^5}$

262. $(9.4 \times 10^6)(3.7 \times 10^5)$

263. $\dfrac{9.46 \times 10^1}{4.4 \times 10^1}$

264. $(7.1 \times 10^2)(6.8 \times 10^1)$

265. $(2 \times 10^6)(5 \times 10^{-6})$

266. $(3.7 \times 10^{-2})(1.8 \times 10^6)$

267. $\dfrac{7 \times 10^3}{4.46 \times 10^{-2}}$

268. $\dfrac{7 \times 10^5}{3.98 \times 10^6}$

269. $(5.2 \times 10^{-6})^2$

270. $(3.4 \times 10^{-1})(2.24 \times 10^2)$

271. $\dfrac{4.8 \times 10^3}{1.3 \times 10^{-3}}$

276. $(4.59 \times 10^1)(6.2 \times 10^2)$

272. $(3.1 \times 10^{-2})(4.3 \times 10^{-4})$

277. $(5.5 \times 10^5)(1.2 \times 10^{-6})$

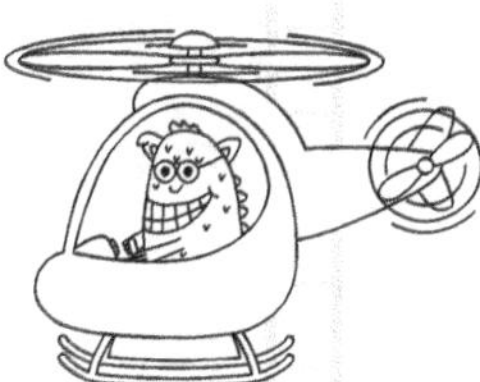

273. $\dfrac{5.1 \times 10^4}{6.2 \times 10^0}$

278. $(4.56 \times 10^3)(4.02 \times 10^{-6})$

274. $\dfrac{4.52 \times 10^{-2}}{2.32 \times 10^{-4}}$

279. $\dfrac{2 \times 10^{-1}}{6.19 \times 10^{-3}}$

275. $(8.24 \times 10^1)(9 \times 10^3)$

280. $(6.8 \times 10^5)^6$

281. $(5.9 \times 10^6)(5.22 \times 10^0)$

282. $(3.2 \times 10^0)(4.43 \times 10^{-2})$

283. $(9.7 \times 10^{-1})(1.28 \times 10^2)$

284. $\dfrac{6 \times 10^4}{5.01 \times 10^{-1}}$

285. $\dfrac{2 \times 10^{-1}}{7 \times 10^{-1}}$

286. $(9.8 \times 10^1)(5.9 \times 10^{-2})$

287. $(6.77 \times 10^{-2})^{-2}$

288. $(8 \times 10^1)(4 \times 10^{-4})$

289. $(2 \times 10^3)(5 \times 10^0)$

290. $(7.31 \times 10^{-4})^{-5}$

291. $\dfrac{6 \times 10^6}{2.6 \times 10^{-3}}$

296. $(8.9 \times 10^2)(7.4 \times 10^{-1})$

292. $(1.4 \times 10^{-1})(4.1 \times 10^1)$

297. $\dfrac{3.8 \times 10^{-3}}{7 \times 10^5}$

293. $\dfrac{9.38 \times 10^{-1}}{4 \times 10^{-3}}$

298. $(2 \times 10^{-2})(9.6 \times 10^{-4})$

294. $(2.42 \times 10^6)(6 \times 10^3)$

299. $\dfrac{5.1 \times 10^5}{6.2 \times 10^5}$

295. $(9.2 \times 10^{-4})^3$

300. $(6.5 \times 10^{-2})(4.3 \times 10^5)$

301. $\dfrac{5.25 \times 10^{-5}}{7.6 \times 10^{-5}}$

302. $\dfrac{9 \times 10^{-2}}{4.57 \times 10^{4}}$

303. $\dfrac{4.12 \times 10^{-3}}{1.7 \times 10^{-4}}$

304. $(1.28 \times 10^{3})^{3}$

305. $(8.9 \times 10^{0})(6 \times 10^{-2})$

306. $(5.53 \times 10^{0})(5 \times 10^{1})$

307. $(4.31 \times 10^{-6})^{-2}$

308. $\dfrac{8.2 \times 10^{-6}}{2.29 \times 10^{5}}$

309. $(6 \times 10^{-6})(9.2 \times 10^{1})$

310. $\dfrac{9.9 \times 10^{-1}}{2 \times 10^{-5}}$

311. $(7.14 \times 10^{-1})^5$

312. $(1.52 \times 10^5)(9.3 \times 10^5)$

313. $(4.87 \times 10^6)(2.3 \times 10^4)$

314. $\dfrac{3.1 \times 10^4}{3 \times 10^0}$

315. $\dfrac{9.3 \times 10^4}{4.8 \times 10^{-5}}$

316. $\dfrac{3.8 \times 10^{-6}}{5 \times 10^1}$

317. $\dfrac{9.98 \times 10^2}{8.2 \times 10^{-2}}$

318. $\dfrac{7.8 \times 10^{-2}}{5.1 \times 10^{-2}}$

319. $\dfrac{1.1 \times 10^0}{5 \times 10^{-3}}$

320. $\dfrac{3.3 \times 10^2}{8 \times 10^{-2}}$

321. $\dfrac{9.5 \times 10^5}{5.3 \times 10^4}$

322. $\dfrac{8.5 \times 10^4}{3.36 \times 10^2}$

323. $(6.2 \times 10^5)^3$

324. $\dfrac{2.85 \times 10^3}{9.57 \times 10^{-6}}$

325. $(5 \times 10^{-5})(8.91 \times 10^{-3})$

326. $(5.5 \times 10^6)(2.52 \times 10^4)$

327. $\dfrac{5 \times 10^5}{7 \times 10^0}$

328. $(8.65 \times 10^{-6})(4.4 \times 10^1)$

329. $(2.7 \times 10^{-2})(5 \times 10^5)$

330. $(7 \times 10^{-5})(7.61 \times 10^1)$

331. $(6 \times 10^4)(8 \times 10^5)$

332. $\dfrac{7 \times 10^2}{3.7 \times 10^5}$

333. $(8 \times 10^4)(4 \times 10^3)$

334. $\dfrac{6.8 \times 10^{-5}}{3.7 \times 10^{-6}}$

335. $(3 \times 10^1)^5$

336. $\dfrac{2.5 \times 10^{-4}}{7 \times 10^0}$

337. $(4.5 \times 10^{-1})(1.9 \times 10^{-1})$

338. $(4.2 \times 10^0)(8.42 \times 10^{-1})$

339. $\dfrac{8 \times 10^3}{6.95 \times 10^6}$

340. $(6.6 \times 10^1)(1.1 \times 10^{-6})$

341. $(3.3 \times 10^2)(2.91 \times 10^3)$

342. $(6.3 \times 10^{-5})(6 \times 10^1)$

343. $\dfrac{6.26 \times 10^3}{7.69 \times 10^3}$

344. $(7.8 \times 10^2)(7.48 \times 10^5)$

345. $(1.4 \times 10^{-4})(1.4 \times 10^2)$

346. $(4.4 \times 10^{-5})(7.5 \times 10^3)$

347. $\dfrac{3.8 \times 10^2}{5.97 \times 10^1}$

348. $(4 \times 10^3)(9.4 \times 10^{-5})$

349. $\dfrac{4 \times 10^{-4}}{3.7 \times 10^{-2}}$

350. $(9.3 \times 10^6)(2 \times 10^{-2})$

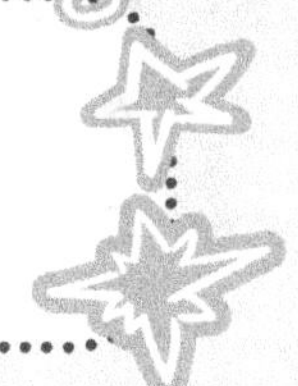

351. $(4.36 \times 10^5)(1.8 \times 10^{-2})$

352. $(6 \times 10^{-3})(1.66 \times 10^0)$

353. $\dfrac{2.7 \times 10^1}{8 \times 10^3}$

354. $\dfrac{6.9 \times 10^4}{3.39 \times 10^{-3}}$

355. $\dfrac{8.53 \times 10^3}{4.02 \times 10^0}$

356. $\dfrac{5.58 \times 10^4}{3.6 \times 10^6}$

357. $\dfrac{6.27 \times 10^3}{3.07 \times 10^{-2}}$

358. $(6.5 \times 10^5)(8.8 \times 10^3)$

359. $\dfrac{1.1 \times 10^3}{3.2 \times 10^{-6}}$

360. $\dfrac{5.8 \times 10^1}{8.01 \times 10^{-6}}$

In this chapter, we will practice solving absolute value equations.

Absolute value equations are mathematical expressions that involve the absolute value of a number or an expression. The absolute value of a number is the **distance** of that number from zero on the number line.

For example, the absolute value of -5 is 5, and the absolute value of 5 is also 5. The symbol for absolute value is two vertical bars, like this: | |.

When solving absolute value equations, the goal is to **isolate** the absolute value expression on one side of the equation, and then split the equation into two separate cases: one where the expression inside the absolute value bars is positive, and one where it is negative. These two cases must be solved separately, as the solution to the absolute value equation is the set of all values that make the equation true.

The process of solving absolute value equations can be broken down into several steps:

1. Remove the absolute value bars: To remove the absolute value bars, we must split the equation into two separate cases: one where the expression inside the absolute value bars is positive, and one where it is negative. For example, if the equation is $|x + 3| = 5$, we can split it into two separate equations: $x + 3 = 5$ and $x + 3 = -5$.

2. Solve each case separately: After splitting the equation into two separate cases, we must solve each case separately. In the first case, $x + 3 = 5$, we can subtract 3 from both sides of the equation to get $x = 2$. In the second case, $x + 3 = -5$, we can again subtract 3 from both sides to get $x = -8$.

3. Check the solutions: Once we have solved both cases, we must check our solutions to ensure that they satisfy the original equation. To do this, we plug our solutions back into the original equation and see if both sides of the equation are equal. If they are equal, our solutions are correct.

4. Write the final solution: The final solution to an absolute value equation is the set of all values that make the equation true. In our example, the final solution is $x = 2$ or $x = -8$.

Guided Practice Question #1:

$$|x - 3| = 3$$

$$x - 3 = 3 \qquad\qquad x - 3 = -3$$
$$+3 \quad +3 \qquad\qquad +3 \quad +3$$
$$\overline{} \qquad\qquad \overline{}$$
$$x = 6 \qquad\qquad x = 0$$

Step 1: We must split the equation into two separate cases: one where the expression inside the absolute value bars is positive, and one where it is negative. **x - 3 = 3** and **x - 3 = -3**.

Step 2: Solve and you see that **x = 6** and **x = 0**.

Guided Practice Question #2:

Step 1: We must split the equation into two separate cases: one where the expression inside the absolute value bars is positive, and one where it is negative.

Step 2: Solve. in this case, we need to multiply both sides by **8.** for the first equation we get a = 16 and the second equation we get a = -16. **The answers are {16, -16}.**

$$\left|\frac{a}{8}\right| = 2$$

$$\frac{a}{8} = 2 \qquad \frac{a}{8} = -2$$

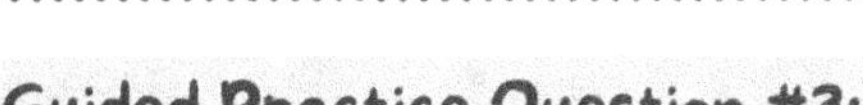

Guided Practice Question #3:

$$|v| + 4 = 6$$

Notice this example is **different** from the previous examples. Remember, that in order to solve for absolute value equations, one of the sides must **ONLY** contain the absolute value expression. In this case we have $|v| + 4$ on the left side. We must get rid of the $+4$ before we split the equation into two different cases. We can easily get rid of the $+4$ by doing the opposite, which is subtract 4 to both sides. This leaves us with $|v| = 2$.

Now, we can split the equations.

$v = 2$ and $v = -2$

Pretty simple! The answers are 2 and -2. Take a look at the next practice example that is slightly more challenging.

Guided Practice Question #4:

$$4\,|n| + 3 = 35$$

Step 1: Subtract 3 from both sides of the equation and we are left with
$4\,|n| = 32$

Step 2: We need to get rid of the 4 on the left side, so we can divide both sides by 4 leaving us with $|n| = 8$

Step 3: Now, we can split the equations.
$n = 8$ and $n = -8$

The answers are 8 and -8.

Guided Practice Question #5:

One final practice question!

$$|6 - 9x| = 39$$

Step 1: We can split the equations. **6 - 9x = 39** and **6 - 9x = -39**

Step 2: Solve both equations

$$6 - 9x = 39$$
$$\underline{-6 \qquad\qquad -6}$$
$$\frac{-9x}{-9} = \frac{33}{-9}$$
$$x = \frac{-33}{9} \text{ or } \frac{-11}{3}$$

and

$$6 - 9x = -39$$
$$\underline{-6 \qquad\qquad -6}$$
$$\frac{-9x}{-9} = \frac{-45}{-9}$$
$$x = 5$$

The answers are $\frac{-11}{3}$ and 5.

Please complete the following practice questions related to solving absolute value equations.

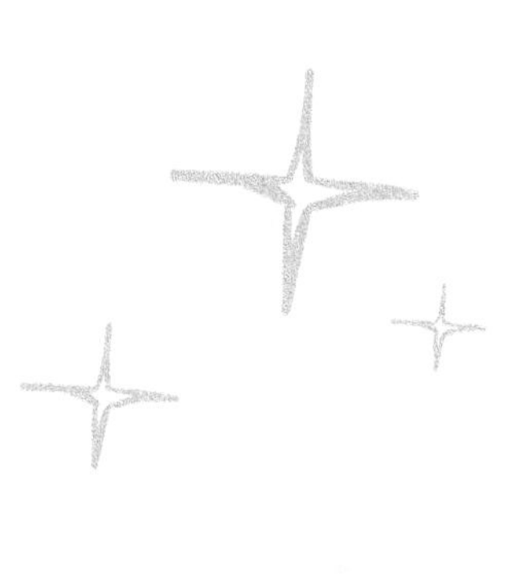

Solve each equation

1. $\left|\dfrac{x}{10}\right| = 2$

2. $|x - 8| = 4$

3. $\left|\dfrac{x}{5}\right| = 2$

4. $|9x| = 36$

5. $|8n| = 48$

6. $|8n| = 64$

7. $\left|\dfrac{x}{5}\right| = 5$

8. $|v + 3| = 7$

9. $|k - 6| = 2$

10. $|x + 5| = 6$

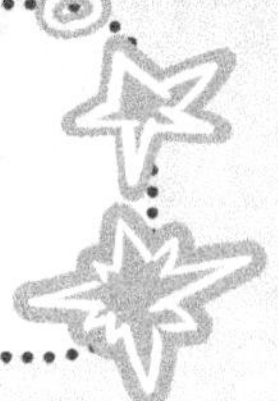

11. $|-5b| = 10$

16. $|-6 + n| = 14$

12. $|x + 9| = 13$

17. $\left|\dfrac{x}{7}\right| = 4$

13. $\left|\dfrac{n}{9}\right| = 5$

18. $\left|\dfrac{b}{3}\right| = 2$

14. $|x - 9| = 7$

19. $|n + 10| = 3$

15. $|-4x| = 40$

20. $|-9 + n| = 4$

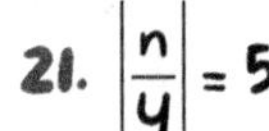

21. $\left|\dfrac{n}{4}\right| = 5$

22. $|n + 9| = 14$

23. $|n - 9| = 14$

24. $|2x| = 20$

25. $|-2b| = 14$

26. $|-6 + x| = 2$

27. $|10b| = 50$

28. $|-6x| = 6$

29. $\left|\dfrac{x}{4}\right| = 3$

30. $\left|\dfrac{k}{2}\right| = 5$

31. $|-6n - 8| = 4$

32. $|-7 - 9m| = 52$

33. $|8 + 5r| = 18$

34. $|8 - 6a| = 40$

35. $|-9 + k| = 9$

36. $|7 + 4b| = 35$

37. $|6 + b| = 3$

38. $|7x + 4| = 66$

39. $|8n - 10| = 2$

40. $|7 + x| = 2$

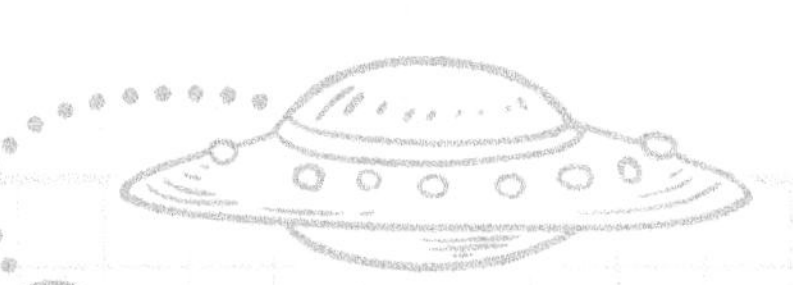

41. $|7 - 5x| = 57$

42. $|9r - 6| = 84$

43. $|4n + 8| = 16$

44. $|4 + 5v| = 49$

45. $|3a - 8| = 13$

46. $|5x + 5| = 35$

47. $|-6n + 3| = 9$

48. $|-8 + 4v| = 20$

49. $|-1 + 4n| = 9$

50. $|5 - x| = 2$

51. $|-1 - 4p| = 23$

52. $|9a - 10| = 37$

53. $|-6n + 10| = 44$

54. $|2 - 2v| = 22$

55. $|10v + 8| = 68$

56. $|4k + 1| = 17$

57. $|5p - 9| = 26$

58. $|7p + 2| = 23$

59. $|3 - 4x| = 27$

60. $|-5b + 10| = 20$

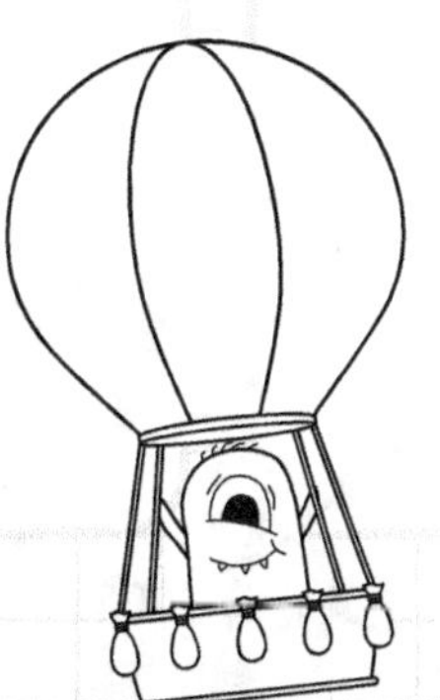

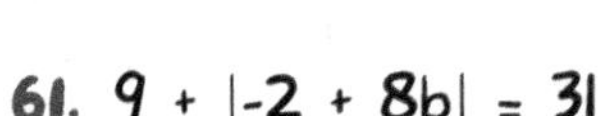

61. $9 + |-2 + 8b| = 31$

66. $|-2 + 9n| - 9 = 38$

62. $|9x - 2| - 4 = 57$

67. $|-v + 3| - 10 = -9$

63. $|8 - 2v| + 7 = 23$

68. $|8n - 10| - 3 = 39$

64. $|9 + 5n| + 2 = 6$

69. $-2|4r - 6| = -68$

65. $-7|2v + 6| = -28$

70. $5 + |-8a - 1| = 78$

71. $\dfrac{|1 - 10n|}{9} = 2$

72. $5 + |5x + 10| = 45$

73. $10|5 - 10x| = 50$

74. $-2|10x - 7| = -26$

75. $-5|3a + 5| = -110$

76. $|5x - 9| - 4 = 10$

77. $\dfrac{|6 - 2x|}{6} = 1$

78. $|10r + 7| + 2 = 79$

79. $9|4n - 4| = 108$

80. $5|1 + 9x| = 85$

81. $-2|-7 - 7x| = -70$

82. $10|-3m + 1| = 110$

83. $|9v + 9| + 9 = 63$

84. $|-k - 10| + 10 = 20$

85. $-4 + |-7x - 6| = 51$

86. $8|10 - 9x| = 64$

87. $\dfrac{|5n - 2|}{2} = 4$

88. $10|2 - 9m| = 20$

89. $|-5x + 5| + 10 = 25$

90. $\dfrac{|x + 1|}{5} = 2$

91. $-4|v| - 7 = -15$

96. $7|b| - 8 = 13$

92. $8|x| - 6 = 18$

97. $2 + 5|p| = 32$

93. $4|r| - 4 = 12$

98. $3|x - 8| = 4$

94. $-5|b| + 6| = -9$

99. $8 - 9|m| = -1$

95. $9|m| + 4 = 58$

100. $10 + |x| = 13$

101. $5|a| - 9 = 16$

102. $|n| + 3 = 10$

103. $6|r| + 3 = 51$

104. $8 - 7|v| = -48$

105. $10|n| + 4 = 94$

106. $10|n| - 5 = 5$

107. $5|m| + 3 = 8$

108. $7 - 2|x| = -13$

109. $10 - |x| = 6$

110. $-2 - 8|x| = -58$

111. $3 - 10|v| = -67$

116. $9|x| + 8 = 53$

112. $8 + 4|b| = 44$

117. $-|x| - 4 = -8$

113. $4 - 3|n| = -11$

118. $-10|b| - 7 = -97$

114. $2|x| + 3 = 19$

119. $6|k| - 4 = 38$

115. $-|a| - 7 = -10$

120. $-3 + 2|x| = -1$

121. $-4|m| - 8 = -24$

122. $|m| - 8 = -6$

123. $9 + 10|n| = 29$

124. $7|r| + 8 = 43$

125. $-8 - 2|n| = -24$

126. $|m| - 6 = -2$

127. $10 - |b| = 1$

128. $-9 - 8|n| = -17$

129. $-8|x| + 7 = -49$

130. $8|r| + 6 = 38$

131. $4|p| + 4 = 36$

132. $4 + 2|n| = 2$

133. $5|k| - 8 = 7$

134. $5|m| - 9 = 21$

135. $2|x| + 1 = 9$

136. $8|b| + 8 = 16$

137. $6|n| + 10 = 46$

138. $9|n| + 10 = 19$

139. $9 + 5|m| = 59$

140. $8 - 5|x| = -7$

141. $-10 + |9x| = 80$

146. $\dfrac{|n+7|}{9} = 4$

142. $|-3n| + 7 = 3$

147. $\dfrac{|x+4|}{6} = 4$

143. $\dfrac{|n-3|}{3} = 4$

148. $\left|\dfrac{k}{3}\right| - 2 = 0$

144. $\dfrac{|-4b|}{9} = 1$

149. $|k|3 - 1 = 7$

145. $\dfrac{|8x|}{4} = 3$

150. $|-9 + p| + 9 = 17$

151. $|6a| + 2 = 38$

156. $-6|b - 6| = -42$

152. $-9 + |r + 9| = -8$

157. $-9 + |n - 7| = -5$

153. $\left|\dfrac{m}{6}\right| + 2 = 3$

158. $\left|\dfrac{x}{3}\right| - 1 = 1$

154. $|8n| - 9 = 39$

159. $\left|\dfrac{a}{3}\right| + 4 = 5$

155. $5 + |-7r| = 75$

160. $\dfrac{|a + 4|}{7} = 5$

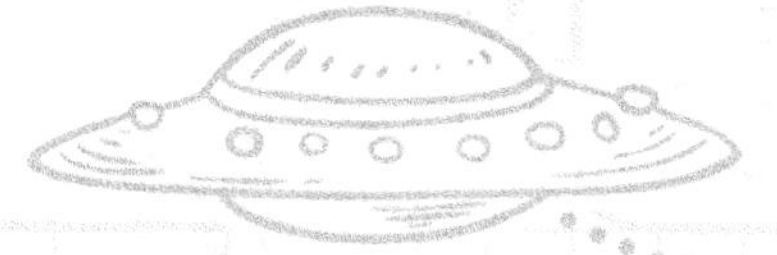

161. $|-8m| - 3 = 21$

166. $\dfrac{|n+1|}{10} = 3$

162. $-9|-4m| = -108$

167. $4|m + 10| = 20$

163. $1 + |n - 9| = 14$

168. $|n + 4| - 7 = 3$

164. $|4x| + 6 = 30$

169. $|n - 10| + 10 = 17$

165. $|m - 6| - 8 = -7$

170. $|-4 + r| - 7 = -3$

171. $\dfrac{|r+5|}{7} = 5$

176. $-10 + |-4k| = -6$

172. $\dfrac{|-9+b|}{9} = 1$

177. $\left|\dfrac{x}{3}\right| - 8 = -7$

173. $\dfrac{|-2x|}{7} = 3$

178. $8|v + 10| = 48$

174. $|6 + p| + 3 = 14$

179. $2|b - 10| = 18$

175. $\dfrac{|-6k|}{8} = 1$

180. $4|a + 5| = 16$

181. $|b - 3| + 6 = 7$

186. $-9|x - 1| = -72$

182. $2 + |m - 6| = 18$

187. $|-1 + x| - 7 = -3$

183. $\dfrac{|9x|}{9} = 2$

188. $-5|x + 8| = -55$

184. $2 + |k + 4| = 16$

189. $10|m - 4| = 30$

185. $3|v + 1| = 30$

190. $|-4n| + 7 = 43$

191. $10 + |9n - 8| = 108$

196. $|-4n + 9| - 6 = 31$

192. $-3|-7a + 3| = -54$

197. $-2 + |7x + 2| = 42$

193. $\dfrac{|8 - 2n|}{8} = 4$

198. $7|8 - 4v| = 28$

194. $|5k - 4| - 2 = 4$

199. $|4m + 2| + 8 = 18$

195. $4|10 + 8x| = 24$

200. $-7|-8 + 2n| = -28$

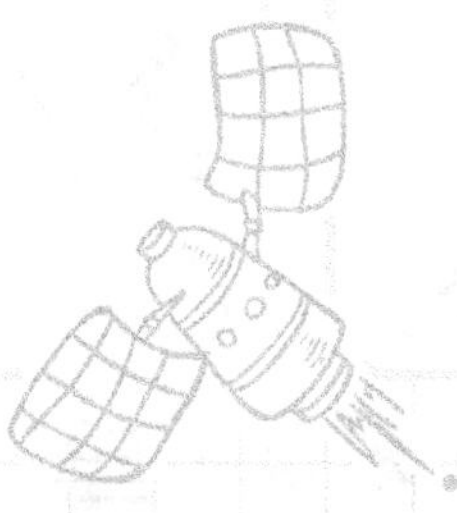

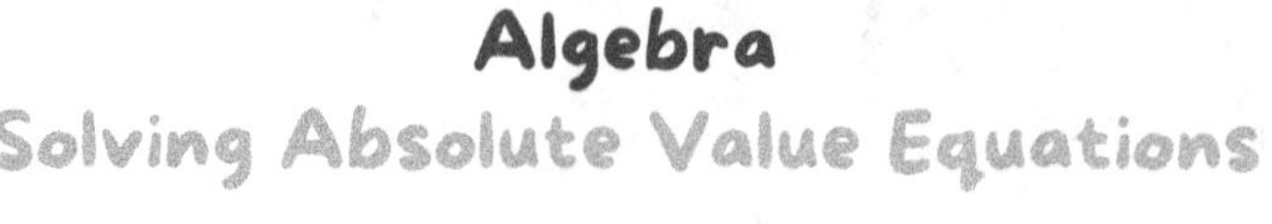

201. $-3 + |-9 - 3b| = 21$

202. $\dfrac{|4 - n|}{6} = 4$

203. $5 + |-6 + 4v| = 27$

204. $9|10 - 5k| = 45$

205. $-10 + |5b + 6| = 9$

206. $|-10a - 8| + 2 = 24$

207. $|9n + 6| - 10 = 65$

208. $\dfrac{|3b - 9|}{6} = 2$

209. $|7x + 6| - 5 = 52$

210. $-2|4x + 6| = -52$

211. $|-3p + 2| - 1 = 28$

216. $|5n + 8| + 3 = 46$

212. $5 + |6 + 5p| = 19$

217. $9 + |6 + 2n| = 11$

213. $|9x - 6| + 3 = 78$

218. $\dfrac{|10 - 8p|}{2} = 4$

214. $5|-5 - 5a| = 100$

219. $|2k + 8| + 6 = 20$

215. $-8|-4m - 6| = -80$

220. $\dfrac{|6x - 1|}{8} = 5$

221. $\dfrac{|-5 - 8x|}{4} = 3$

226. $|-3 + v| + 1 = 13$

222. $-10 + |5 - 6x| = 25$

227. $-5|-m - 6| = -15$

223. $-8|3b - 5| = -112$

228. $7|8 + n| = 7$

224. $\dfrac{|-9n + 9|}{6} = 4$

229. $|5 - 8x| - 7 = 44$

225. $5 + |-2a + 6| = 19$

230. $2 + |7n + 8| = 57$

231. $|10 + 3b| - 2 = 38$

236. $|5n - 9| - 3 = 18$

232. $|5v - 8| + 2 = 60$

237. $|8x + 5| - 9 = 68$

233. $\dfrac{|6x + 3|}{9} = 2$

238. $\dfrac{|5a - 6|}{8} = 1$

234. $5 + |8b - 3| = 80$

239. $|2v - 9| - 10 = -7$

235. $4 + |6x - 4| = 56$

240. $|5x - 4| - 5 = 44$

241. $\dfrac{|-2-5n|}{6} = 1$

242. $7|-1 + 6b| = 49$

243. $2 + |6 + 4m| = 12$

244. $-3 + |-8b + 4| = 65$

245. $|-4m - 3| - 4 = 11$

246. $\dfrac{|10 + 7x|}{9} = 3$

247. $\dfrac{|8k + 10|}{4} = 3$

248. $\dfrac{|2 + 10x|}{4} = 3$

249. $\dfrac{|-5x - 4|}{10} = 3$

250. $8 + |5x - 1| = 39$

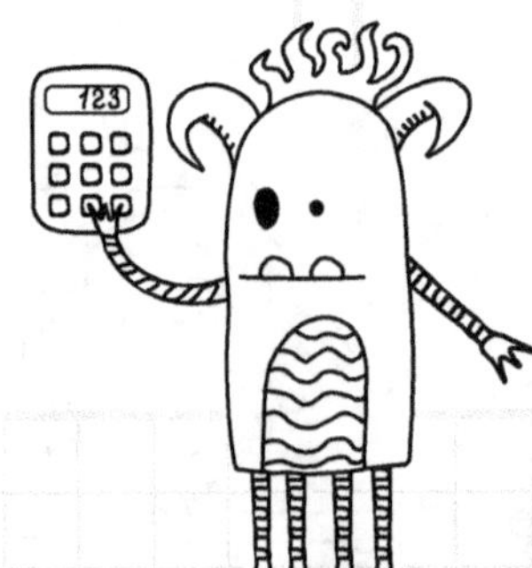

251. $|4a - 6| - 10 = 28$

256. $\dfrac{|3b + 8|}{5} = 1$

252. $|8r - 6| + 5 = 39$

257. $8 + |8 + 10r| = 16$

253. $|-9 + 7x| - 5 = 14$

258. $-4 + |6m - 3| = 17$

254. $5|4 + 10n| = 30$

259. $|10n - 9| - 5 = 34$

255. $|5p - 9| + 3 = 29$

260. $-9 + |2k - 8| = 17$

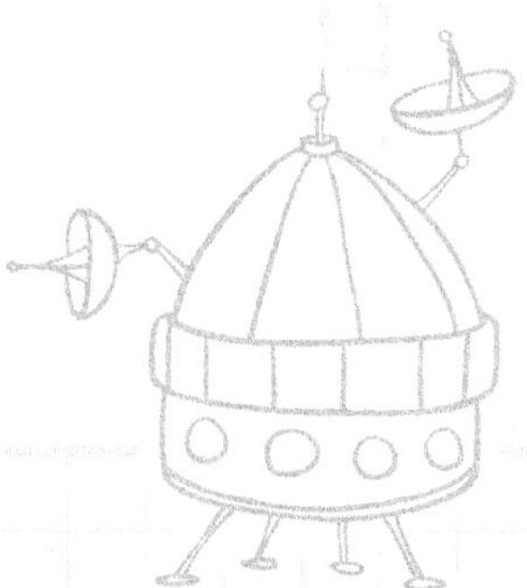

261. $-4\,|-4x - 9| = -108$

262. $-7|-4x - 1| = -119$

263. $|m - 6| - 4 = 8$

264. $-4|-10 - 3k| = -56$

265. $\dfrac{|4k - 5|}{7} = 3$

266. $\dfrac{|-9 - 3a|}{2} = 2$

267. $-7|10x - 7| = -91$

268. $|6r - 7| + 2 = 21$

269. $\dfrac{|9x + 8|}{3} = 4$

270. $\dfrac{|4n + 10|}{3} = 5$

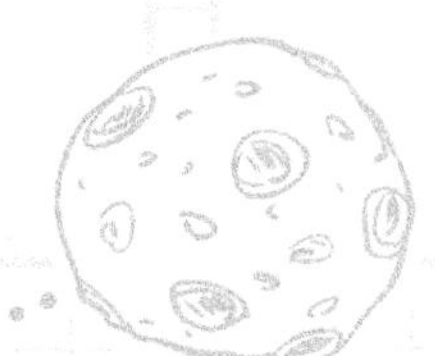

271. $-4|-7 + 6r| = -116$

276. $7|6 - 3p| = 42$

272. $|-9 + 2r| + 6 = 23$

277. $|4 + 3x| + 9 = 25$

273. $5 + |1 - 7r| = 32$

278. $|6 - 5n| + 5 = 46$

274. $|6x - 9| + 4 = 13$

279. $4|6n + 7| = 76$

275. $\dfrac{|-10r - 9|}{3} = 4$

280. $-3|6 + 5n| = -63$

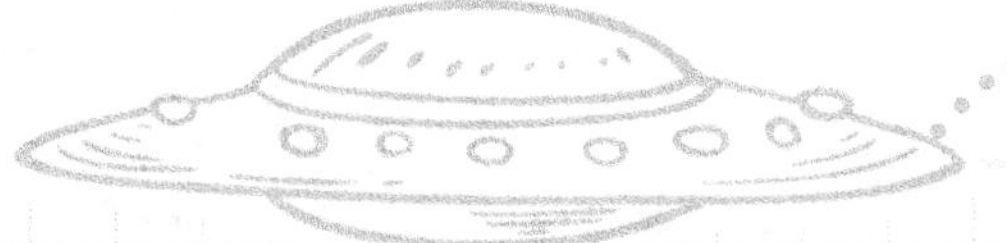

281. $-3|8 + 9x| = -111$

282. $|3p + 6| - 10 = -7$

283. $\dfrac{|7v + 5|}{5} = 4$

284. $4|-10x - 9| = 116$

285. $|10 - 2n| + 5 = 7$

286. $|-2r - 4| + 4 = 16$

287. $|2 + 9n| + 7 = 99$

288. $6|2x - 4| = 24$

289. $4|10b + 9| = 44$

290. $-7|x - 3| = -28$

291. $\dfrac{|-2 + 2x|}{5} = 4$

292. $10|-9 + 2r| = 30$

293. $-3|4x + 5| = -57$

294. $|2 + 10a| + 10 = 38$

295. $|10n + 3| - 3 = 54$

296. $8|2n + 6| = 32$

297. $\dfrac{|4x - 2|}{8} = 3$

298. $|10 + 2p| - 10 = -4$

299. $-9 + |-6n - 8| = 7$

300. $\dfrac{|7 + 5r|}{5} = 5$

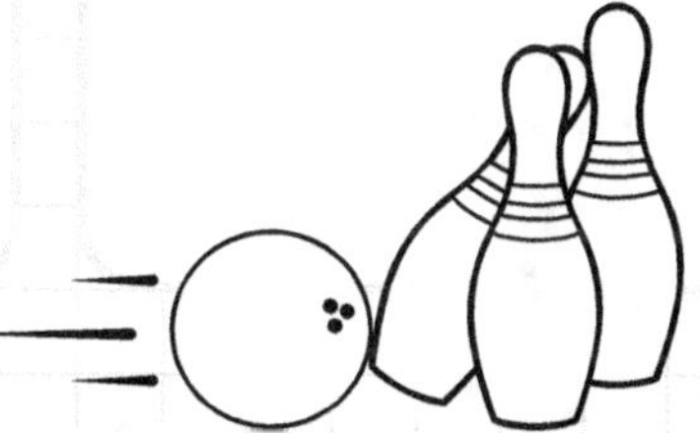

Quadratic equations are equations of the form **$ax^2 + bx + c = 0$**, where **a, b,** and **c** are **constants**, and **x** is the **variable**. A quadratic equation can have two solutions, one solution, or no real solutions at all. In this chapter, we will focus on solving quadratic equations by factoring, which is one of the most popular and effective methods for solving quadratic equations.

There are three basic methods for solving quadratic equations: factoring, using the quadratic formula, and completing the square.

Factoring is the process of finding the factors of a polynomial. In the case of quadratic equations, factoring involves finding two numbers that multiply to give the constant term c and add to give the coefficient of the x-term b. Once these numbers are found, the quadratic equation can be factored into two linear factors, and the roots of the quadratic equation can be obtained by setting each factor equal to zero.

Using the factoring method is easy and fast when you are working with quadratic equations where there the coefficient of "a" is 1.

Here are a few quadratic equations that can be solved by factoring.

$$x^2 + 4x - 45 = 0$$

$$x^2 - 16x + 48 = 0$$

$$x^2 - 20x - 69 = 0$$

*Notice that the coefficient of x^2 in all three equations above are 1.

Let's take a look at the steps for solving a quadratic equation by factoring.

Step 1: Write the quadratic equation in standard form: **$ax^2 + bx + c = 0$.**

In this chapter, all of the practice questions you will focus on have already been arranged and written for you in the standard form.

Step 2: Factor the quadratic equation.

Factor the constant term c into two numbers that multiply to give c and add to give the coefficient of the x-term b.

Step 3: Rewrite the quadratic equation as a product of two linear factors: $(x + q)(x + s) = 0$, where q and s are constants.

Step 4: Set each factor equal to zero and solve for x.

Let's take an example to understand this method more clearly.

$x^2 + 3x - 4 = 0$

Let's go ahead and write $(x + q)(x + s) = 0$

I know I need to find out what "q" and "s" is.

Remember we need "q" and "s" to multiply to give us the constant (c) . The constant in this equation is -4.

At the same time, we also need "q" and "s" to add up to give us the coefficient of the x-term b, which is 3.

Let's think: What 2 numbers multiply to -4?

Some possible answers include -4 and 1, -1 and 4, 2 and -2

From those possible answers, which of those also add to 3?

The numbers -1 and 4 add to 3.

The numbers -1 and 4 are the constants "p" and "s". Let"s plug that back into $(x + q)(x + s) = 0$

We have $(x - 1)(x + 4) = 0$

Now, let's set each factor equal to zero and solve for x.

We have $x - 1 = 0$ which gives us $x = 1$ and we have $x + 4 = 0$ which gives us $x = -4$.

We call these answers the roots of the quadratic equation. So the roots of this quadratic equation is $x = 1$ and $x = -4$.

Finally we can double-check our work by plugging these values back into our original quadratic equation to see if it's true.

$$(1)^2 + 3(1) - 4 = 0 \qquad\qquad (-4)^2 + 3(-4) - 4 = 0$$
$$1 + 3 - 4 = 0 \quad \& \quad 16 - 12 - 4 = 0$$
$$\textbf{TRUE} \qquad\qquad\qquad \textbf{TRUE}$$

We just double-checked our work and verified that both these answers are correct!

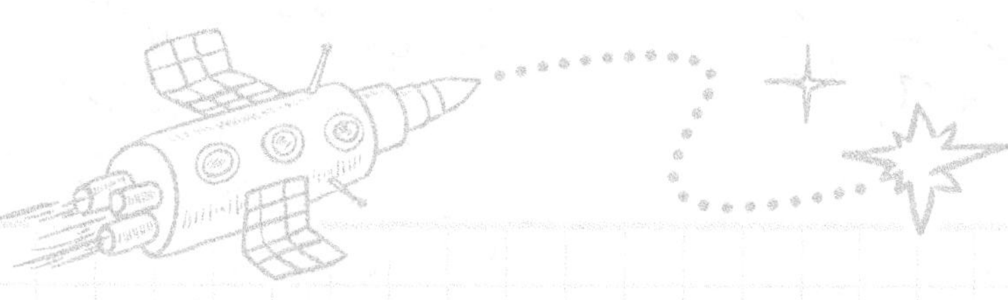

Let's try a few more guided practice questions.

Guided Practice Question #1:

$x^2 + 3x - 10 = 0$

Condition # 1:

Multiply two numbers to get this...

$$x^2 + 3x - 10 = 0$$

Condition # 2:

Add two numbers to get this...

$(x + q)(x + s) = 0$

What two numbers multiply to -10 but also add to 3?

That would be **5** and **-2**. Plug those numbers in.

$(x + 5)(x - 2) = 0$

Now let's set each factor equal to zero and solve for x.

We have $x + 5 = 0$, which if we solve for x, we get $x = -5$.

We also have $x - 2 = 0$, which if we solve for x, we get $x = 2$.

So the final solutions are $x = -5$ and **2**. If you plug these numbers back into the quadratic equation, you will see the solutions are valid.

Guided Practice Question #2:

$x^2 - x - 42 = 0$

Which two numbers multiply to -42 but also add to -1?

That would be 6 and -7.

So we have $(x + 6)(x - 7) = 0$

Solve for x.

You get the two solutions $x = -6$ and 7.

$$x^2 - x - 42 = 0$$
$$(x + 6)(x - 7) = 0$$
$$x + 6 = 0 \quad \text{or} \quad x - 7 = 0$$

$$x + 6 - 6 = 0 - 6 \qquad x - 7 + 7 = 0 + 7$$
$$x = -6 \qquad\qquad x = 7$$

Guided Practice Question #3:

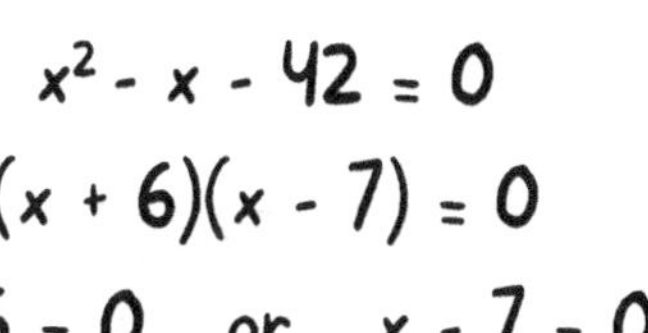

$$\text{Solve } x^2 - 8x + 15 = 0$$
$$(x - 3)(x - 5) = 0$$

$$x - 3 = 0 \qquad x - 5 = 0$$
$$x = 3 \qquad\quad x = 5$$

The solutions are $x = 3$ and $x = 5$.

Great work. Go ahead and try the following practice questions using this method.

Solve each quadratic equation

1. $m^2 + 10m + 9 = 0$

6. $m^2 + 6m - 7 = 0$

2. $x^2 + 10x - 39 = 0$

7. $x^2 + 2x - 8 = 0$

3. $p^2 - 18p + 56 = 0$

8. $n^2 - 18n - 40 = 0$

4. $x^2 - 16x + 48 = 0$

9. $r^2 - 16r - 57 = 0$

5. $a^2 - 16a + 55 = 0$

10. $x^2 + 12x - 45 = 0$

11. $r^2 + 12r + 27 = 0$

12. $m^2 - 18m + 77 = 0$

13. $b^2 - 4b - 32 = 0$

14. $n^2 + 14n + 45 = 0$

15. $x^2 - 16x + 39 = 0$

16. $a^2 + 2a - 35 = 0$

17. $p^2 + 16p + 55 = 0$

18. $k^2 - 12k - 64 = 0$

19. $x^2 + 10x - 96 = 0$

20. $v^2 + 20v + 36 = 0$

21. $x^2 - 14x - 32 = 0$

26. $r^2 - 6r - 55 = 0$

22. $b^2 - 18b - 19 = 0$

27. $k^2 + 14k - 51 = 0$

23. $x^2 - 12x + 32 = 0$

28. $b^2 + 2b - 48 = 0$

24. $a^2 - 8a - 84 = 0$

29. $r^2 + 8r + 15 = 0$

25. $x^2 - 2x - 99 = 0$

30. $m^2 + 10m + 24 = 0$

31. $b^2 + 12b + 32 = 0$

32. $n^2 - 18n - 88 = 0$

33. $k^2 + 20k - 21 = 0$

34. $a^2 + 14a - 95 = 0$

35. $x^2 - 4x - 45 = 0$

36. $x^2 - 6x - 72 = 0$

37. $b^2 + 8b - 33 = 0$

38. $n^2 + 12n + 11 = 0$

39. $m^2 + 18m - 63 = 0$

40. $r^2 - 10r - 24 = 0$

41. $n^2 - 6n - 27 = 0$

42. $a^2 - 14a + 24 = 0$

43. $x^2 - 2x - 24 = 0$

44. $a^2 - 6a - 91 = 0$

45. $m^2 - 16m - 80 = 0$

46. $m^2 + 16m + 63 = 0$

47. $x^2 - 16x + 28 = 0$

48. $r^2 - 4r - 5 = 0$

49. $x^2 - 18x + 32 = 0$

50. $n^2 - 8n + 12 = 0$

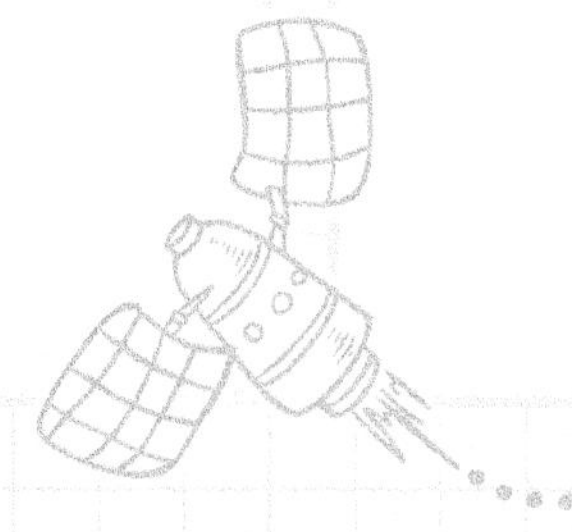

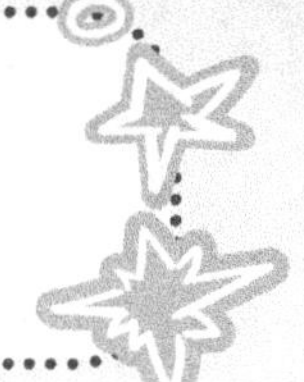

51. $x^2 + 18x + 56 = 0$

52. $x^2 + 16x + 39 = 0$

53. $a^2 - 2a - 15 = 0$

54. $m^2 - 20m + 99 = 0$

55. $n^2 - 14n + 48 = 0$

56. $a^2 + 18a + 77 = 0$

57. $n^2 - 16n + 63 = 0$

58. $n^2 + 4n - 60 = 0$

59. $k^2 + 8k - 48 = 0$

60. $n^2 - 10n - 96 = 0$

61. $n^2 + 10n + 16 = 0$

66. $p^2 + 8p - 20 = 0$

62. $n^2 - 10n - 75 = 0$

67. $n^2 - 14n - 72 = 0$

63. $x^2 - 10x - 39 = 0$

68. $a^2 + 12a - 85 = 0$

64. $b^2 - 20b - 96 = 0$

69. $b^2 + 18b - 19 = 0$

65. $m^2 + 10m - 75 = 0$

70. $x^2 - 8x - 33 = 0$

71. $p^2 + 2p - 63 = 0$

72. $r^2 + 18r + 80 = 0$

73. $v^2 - 12v - 13 = 0$

74. $b^2 - 20b - 69 = 0$

75. $b^2 - 6b + 8 = 0$

76. $n^2 - 18n + 45 = 0$

77. $x^2 - 14x + 33 = 0$

78. $b^2 + 8b + 7 = 0$

79. $p^2 - 20p + 36 = 0$

80. $x^2 + 6x - 91 = 0$

81. $m^2 + 4m - 96 = 0$

82. $n^2 - 10n + 9 = 0$

83. $k^2 + 14k - 32 = 0$

84. $p^2 + 10p - 24 = 0$

85. $x^2 - 12x - 45 = 0$

86. $p^2 + 14p + 40 = 0$

87. $b^2 + 6b + 8 = 0$

88. $n^2 + 8n - 65 = 0$

89. $p^2 + 20p + 64 = 0$

90. $x^2 + 18x + 72 = 0$

91. $x^2 + 18x + 65 = 0$

92. $v^2 + 10v - 56 = 0$

93. $n^2 + 14n + 48 = 0$

94. $b^2 + 14b - 15 = 0$

95. $k^2 - 2k - 35 = 0$

96. $x^2 + 12x - 28 = 0$

97. $r^2 + 16r + 60 = 0$

98. $r^2 + 8r - 84 = 0$

99. $x^2 + 14x + 24 = 0$

100. $n^2 + 10n + 9 = 0$

101. $b^2 - 10b - 75 = 0$

102. $m^2 + 14m - 72 = 0$

103. $p^2 - 4p - 96 = 0$

104. $m^2 + 8m - 9 = 0$

105. $x^2 + 14x + 13 = 0$

106. $x^2 + 8x - 84 = 0$

107. $b^2 + 2b - 48 = 0$

108. $x^2 + 6x - 40 = 0$

109. $m^2 + 18m - 88 = 0$

110. $r^2 + 10r + 21 = 0$

111. $n^2 - 8n + 7 = 0$

112. $r^2 - 8r - 65 = 0$

113. $v^2 - 18v + 17 = 0$

114. $x^2 + 20x + 75 = 0$

115. $x^2 + 16x + 28 = 0$

116. $x^2 - 12x - 85 = 0$

117. $k^2 - 20k - 69 = 0$

118. $x^2 - 14x + 45 = 0$

119. $n^2 - 4n - 32 = 0$

120. $b^2 - 14b + 24 = 0$

121. $k^2 + 2k - 80 = 0$

122. $r^2 + 6r - 16 = 0$

123. $x^2 + 18x + 32 = 0$

124. $x^2 - 16x + 48 = 0$

125. $n^2 + 10n - 39 = 0$

126. $x^2 + 2x - 63 = 0$

127. $n^2 + 14n - 32 = 0$

128. $k^2 + 6k - 91 = 0$

129. $x^2 + 4x - 45 = 0$

130. $n^2 + 18n - 40 = 0$

131. $p^2 + 14p + 48 = 0$

132. $x^2 + 16x + 63 = 0$

133. $x^2 + 12x + 35 = 0$

134. $x^2 + 18x + 17 = 0$

135. $b^2 + 14b + 24 = 0$

136. $m^2 - 4m + 3 = 0$

137. $x^2 - 4x - 45 = 0$

138. $n^2 - 12n + 32 = 0$

139. $a^2 + 6a - 7 = 0$

140. $a^2 - 14a - 51 = 0$

141. $x^2 - 4x - 5 = 0$

142. $x^2 - 16x + 60 = 0$

143. $x^2 + 10x - 75 = 0$

144. $b^2 - 4b - 21 = 0$

145. $n^2 - 14n - 15 = 0$

146. $n^2 + 4n + 3 = 0$

147. $n^2 + 14n + 40 = 0$

148. $b^2 - 4b - 12 = 0$

149. $n^2 - 20n - 21 = 0$

150. $x^2 - 18x - 19 = 0$

151. $x^2 + 20x + 51 = 0$

152. $x^2 - 2x - 8 = 0$

153. $r^2 + 18r + 45 = 0$

154. $v^2 - 12v + 11 = 0$

155. $p^2 - 12p + 20 = 0$

156. $n^2 - 2n - 48 = 0$

157. $n^2 + 16n + 55 = 0$

158. $x^2 - 6x - 55 = 0$

159. $x^2 + 12x - 13 = 0$

160. $p^2 + 2p - 8 = 0$

161. $n^2 + 16n - 57 = 0$

162. $v^2 - 18v + 80 = 0$

163. $r^2 - 12r + 27 = 0$

164. $k^2 - 10k + 16 = 0$

165. $n^2 - 2n - 80 = 0$

166. $n^2 - 12n + 35 = 0$

167. $a^2 + 6a - 72 = 0$

168. $x^2 + 10x - 96 = 0$

169. $n^2 - 20n + 75 = 0$

170. $b^2 - 12b - 13 = 0$

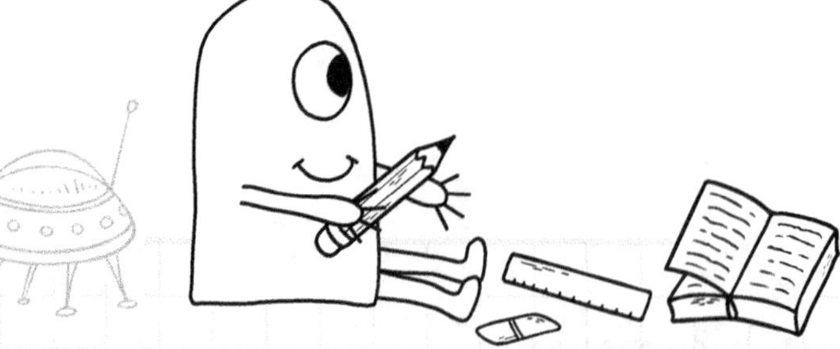

171. $p^2 - 4p - 60 = 0$

176. $r^2 + 6r + 8 = 0$

172. $x^2 - 18x + 56 = 0$

177. $x^2 - 8x + 12 = 0$

173. $n^2 - 20n - 96 = 0$

178. $b^2 + 18b + 56 = 0$

174. $m^2 + 20m + 19 = 0$

179. $x^2 + 2x - 3 = 0$

175. $x^2 + 4x - 60 = 0$

180. $x^2 - 20x + 36 = 0$

181. $x^2 - 6x - 7 = 0$

182. $a^2 - 14a + 48 = 0$

183. $n^2 + 8n + 12 = 0$

184. $v^2 - 10v + 24 = 0$

185. $k^2 + 20k - 21 = 0$

186. $x^2 - 10x - 11 = 0$

187. $r^2 + 20r - 96 = 0$

188. $b^2 - 14b - 72 = 0$

189. $r^2 + 6r + 5 = 0$

190. $n^2 + 18n + 77 = 0$

191. $a^2 + 14a + 33 = 0$

196. $x^2 - 6x + 5 = 0$

192. $p^2 + 8p - 48 = 0$

197. $a^2 + 18a + 65 = 0$

193. $x^2 - 6x - 91 = 0$

198. $p^2 - 8p - 20 = 0$

194. $x^2 - 16x + 63 = 0$

199. $a^2 + 8a - 84 = 0$

195. $x^2 + 20x + 36 = 0$

200. $n^2 - 12n - 13 = 0$

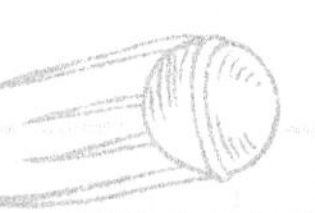

201. $r^2 - 12r + 35 = 0$

202. $b^2 + 20b - 21 = 0$

203. $b^2 + 12b + 20 = 0$

204. $p^2 + 14p - 51 = 0$

205. $a^2 - 16a - 17 = 0$

206. $n^2 - 16n - 80 = 0$

207. $x^2 - 8x - 48 = 0$

208. $x^2 - 12x - 85 = 0$

209. $a^2 - 14a + 24 = 0$

210. $n^2 - 8n + 12 = 0$

211. $b^2 - 18b + 45 = 0$

216. $a^2 + 8a - 33 = 0$

212. $v^2 - 4v - 45 = 0$

217. $b^2 - 4b - 60 = 0$

213. $x^2 + 12x - 85 = 0$

218. $x^2 + 18x + 65 = 0$

214. $m^2 - 2m - 15 = 0$

219. $n^2 + 10n + 16 = 0$

215. $p^2 + 6p - 55 = 0$

220. $n^2 - 18n - 19 = 0$

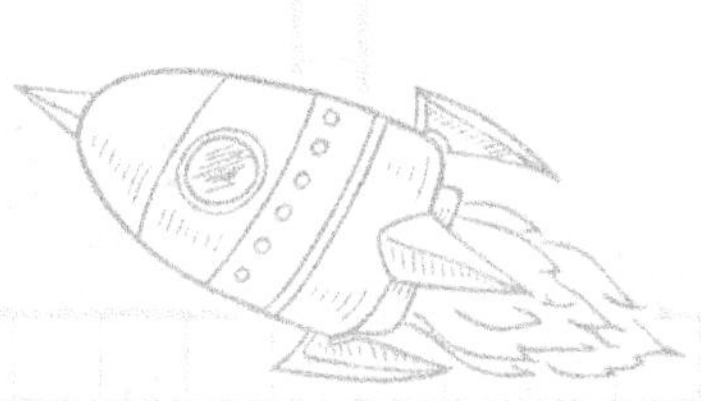

221. $v^2 - 10v - 75 = 0$

222. $r^2 - 18r - 63 = 0$

223. $n^2 + 2n - 80 = 0$

224. $x^2 - 14x + 45 = 0$

225. $p^2 + 12p - 64 = 0$

226. $n^2 - 14n + 33 = 0$

227. $n^2 - 10n + 16 = 0$

228. $a^2 + 20a + 36 = 0$

229. $n^2 - 4n - 5 = 0$

230. $r^2 - 4r - 21 = 0$

231. $n^2 + 10n - 24 = 0$

236. $n^2 - 10n - 24 = 0$

232. $a^2 - 2a - 80 = 0$

237. $x^2 + 16x + 15 = 0$

233. $x^2 + 16x + 55 = 0$

238. $k^2 + 6k + 5 = 0$

234. $r^2 - 6r - 7 = 0$

239. $b^2 + 12b + 35 = 0$

235. $x^2 + 8x + 15 = 0$

240. $n^2 + 14n + 48 = 0$

241. $v^2 - 18v + 72 = 0$

242. $n^2 + 14n + 40 = 0$

243. $x^2 - 16x + 60 = 0$

244. $r^2 - 2r - 35 = 0$

245. $r^2 + 8r - 20 = 0$

246. $x^2 + 12x - 13 = 0$

247. $n^2 + 8n + 12 = 0$

248. $x^2 - 12x - 45 = 0$

249. $p^2 - 18p + 80 = 0$

250. $p^2 - 16p + 39 = 0$

251. $n^2 + 14n + 13 = 0$

252. $x^2 + 18x + 77 = 0$

253. $x^2 + 16x + 63 = 0$

254. $k^2 - 14k + 48 = 0$

255. $x^2 - 16x + 15 = 0$

256. $v^2 - 8v - 65 = 0$

257. $n^2 + 4n + 3 = 0$

258. $x^2 - 10x - 56 = 0$

259. $n^2 + 8n - 9 = 0$

260. $n^2 + 14n + 33 = 0$

261. $n^2 + 18n + 45 = 0$

266. $v^2 + 14v + 24 = 0$

262. $x^2 + 10x - 75 = 0$

267. $a^2 + 4a - 96 = 0$

263. $x^2 + 16x + 28 = 0$

268. $x^2 + 20x + 96 = 0$

264. $x^2 - 12x - 28 = 0$

269. $a^2 + 20a + 91 = 0$

265. $m^2 - 4m - 96 = 0$

270. $b^2 - 4b + 3 = 0$

271. $v^2 + 2v - 63 = 0$

272. $x^2 - 10x - 11 = 0$

273. $k^2 + 12k + 32 = 0$

274. $r^2 + 6r - 16 = 0$

275. $x^2 + 2x - 48 = 0$

276. $p^2 + 4p - 60 = 0$

277. $m^2 + 10m - 39 = 0$

278. $n^2 - 12n + 20 = 0$

279. $v^2 + 6v - 72 = 0$

280. $n^2 - 6n + 5 = 0$

281. $n^2 + 8n + 7 = 0$

286. $a^2 + 14a - 32 = 0$

282. $m^2 + 6m - 91 = 0$

287. $n^2 + 20n + 75 = 0$

283. $v^2 + 2v - 99 = 0$

288. $v^2 - 14v + 13 = 0$

284. $m^2 - 14m + 40 = 0$

289. $a^2 + 10a + 9 = 0$

285. $p^2 - 12p + 11 = 0$

290. $x^2 + 18x - 19 = 0$

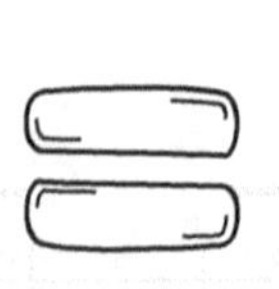

291. $v^2 + 10v - 96 = 0$

292. $p^2 - 8p - 84 = 0$

293. $p^2 - 4p - 32 = 0$

294. $p^2 - 6p - 16 = 0$

295. $n^2 + 12n + 11 = 0$

296. $p^2 + 2p - 8 = 0$

297. $k^2 + 14k - 15 = 0$

298. $k^2 - 14k + 33 = 0$

299. $b^2 + 18b - 63 = 0$

300. $x^2 + 18x + 45 = 0$

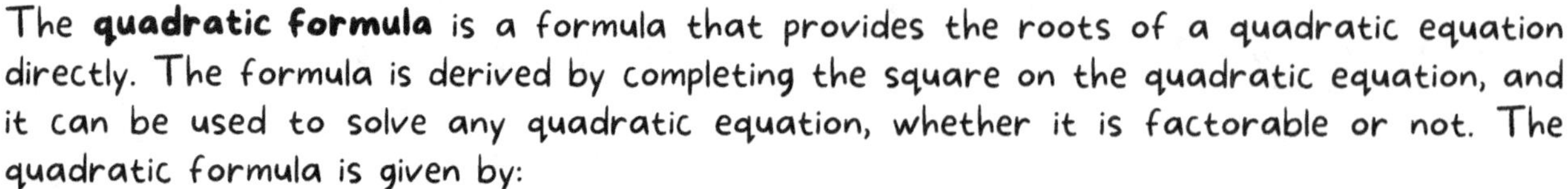

The **quadratic formula** is a formula that provides the roots of a quadratic equation directly. The formula is derived by completing the square on the quadratic equation, and it can be used to solve any quadratic equation, whether it is factorable or not. The quadratic formula is given by:

$$x = \frac{-b \pm \sqrt{(b^2 - 4ac)}}{2a}$$

where a, b, and c are the coefficients of the quadratic equation in standard form.

The steps to solve a quadratic equation by using the quadratic formula are as follows:

Step 1: Write the quadratic equation in standard form: $ax^2 + bx + c = 0$.

Step 2: Identify the coefficients a, b, and c.

Step 3: Substitute the coefficients into the quadratic formula.

Step 4: Simplify the expression inside the square root.

Step 5: Evaluate the expression and simplify the roots.

Let's take a look at the example
$2x^2 - 4x - 30 = 0$.
Let's use the Quadratic Formula to solve.

Solve $2x^2 - 4x - 30 = 0$, $a = 2$, $b = -4$, $c = -30$

$$x = \frac{-b \pm \sqrt{b^2 - 4ac}}{2a}$$

$$x = \frac{4 \pm \sqrt{-4^2 - 4 \times 2 \times (-30)}}{2 \times 2}$$

$$x = \frac{4 \pm \sqrt{16 + 240}}{4}$$

$$x = \frac{4 \pm \sqrt{256}}{4} = \frac{4 \pm 16}{4}$$

$$x_1 = \frac{4 + 16}{4} = 5 \qquad x_2 = \frac{4 - 16}{4} = -3$$

The solutions to the above quadratic equations are $x = 5$ and and $x = -3$.

Let's look at another example.

$x^2 + 4x + 3 = 0$

Use quadratic formula with $a = 1$, $b = 4$, $c = 3$

$$x = \frac{-b \pm \sqrt{b^2 - 4ac}}{2a}$$

$$x = \frac{-(4) \pm \sqrt{(4)^2 - 4(1)(3)}}{2(1)}$$

$$x = \frac{-4 \pm \sqrt{4}}{2}$$

$$\boxed{x = -1 \text{ or } x = -3}$$

The solutions to the above quadratic equations are $x = -1$ and $x = -3$.

How about $2x^2 = -9x + 5$?

Notice that we must make sure that the equation is in standard form which is $ax^2 + bx + c = 0$. So we need to re-write this as $2x^2 + 9x - 5 = 0$.

Now we can solve, $a = 2$, $b = 9$, and $c = -5$.

$$x = \frac{-b \pm \sqrt{b^2 - 4ac}}{2a}$$

$$x = \frac{-9 \pm \sqrt{9^2 - 4 \times 2 \times (-5)}}{2 \times 2}$$

$$x = \frac{-9 \pm \sqrt{81 - (-40)}}{4}$$

$$x = \frac{-9 \pm \sqrt{121}}{4}$$

$$x = \frac{-9 \pm 11}{4}$$

$$x = \frac{-9 + 11}{4} \qquad x = \frac{-9 - 11}{4}$$

$$x = \frac{2}{4} = \frac{1}{2} \qquad x = \frac{-20}{4} = -5$$

The solutions to the above quadratic equations are $x = \frac{1}{2}$ and $x = -5$.
Try the following questions on your own.

Solve each equation with the quadratic formula

1. 1) $x^2 + 2x = 80$

2. $b^2 - 3b = 88$

3. $6n^2 - 32 = 4n$

4. $2k^2 + 4k = 96$

5. $a^2 - 40 = -3a$

6. $a^2 = -12a - 27$

7. $4x^2 = 120 - 4x$

8. $x^2 + 7x = 60$

9. $p^2 = -18 + 11p$

10. $v^2 = 8v + 128$

11. $m^2 - 7m = 60$

16. $4b^2 - 36 = -7b$

12. $4b^2 + 4 = 10b$

17. $x^2 - 2x = 80$

13. $a^2 - 8a = 33$

18. $v^2 = 133 - 12v$

14. $r^2 - 18 = 3r$

19. $x^2 - 24 = 10x$

15. $b^2 - 4b = 96$

20. $4x^2 + 3x = 1$

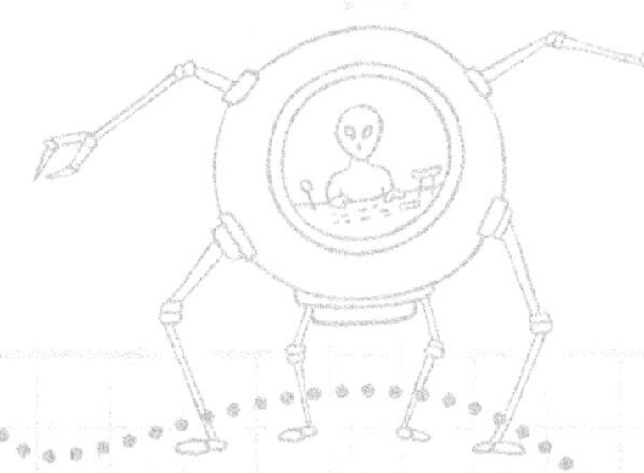

21. $2b^2 - 6b = 56$

26. $n^2 = n + 56$

22. $2m^2 = -11m - 5$

27. $2b^2 - 16 = 4b$

23. $b^2 - 9b = -18$

28. $2a^2 - 8a = 24$

24. $4p^2 - 12p = 16$

29. $3x^2 - 44 = -x$

25. $r^2 - 8r = -15$

30. $n^2 - 11 = -10n$

31. $5m^2 - 6m = -1$

36. $3b^2 = -3b + 6$

32. $2x^2 - 12 = 2x$

37. $2r^2 - 3 = 5r$

33. $v^2 - 4 = 3v$

38. $x^2 - 2x = 99$

34. $4k^2 - 12k = 40$

39. $x^2 + 6 = -7x$

35. $a^2 - 5a = 66$

40. $m^2 - 65 = -8m$

41. $2b^2 - 72 = -10b$

42. $4n^2 = 72 - 12n$

43. $x^2 = -9x + 112$

44. $2n^2 = 132 + 10n$

45. $x^2 + 6x = 55$

46. $k^2 = -7k + 18$

47. $4x^2 = 32 - 8x$

48. $6x^2 - x = 1$

49. $6n^2 + 6n = 36$

50. $5n^2 = 10n + 120$

51. $2x^2 - 2x = 84$

56. $6n^2 + n = 126$

52. $k^2 - 12 = 4k$

57. $4n^2 - 2n = 56$

53. $2p^2 = 48 - 4p$

58. $2p^2 = 10 + 8p$

54. $6n^2 - 30 = 8n$

59. $2k^2 = 3k + 135$

55. $3r^2 - 60 = 3r$

60. $4a^2 - 3a = 27$

61. $5x^2 = 72 + 2x$

66. $3a^2 = 5a + 78$

62. $5x^2 - 144 = -6x$

67. $6b^2 = -10b + 136$

63. $6x^2 = 11x + 10$

68. $6v^2 - 34 = -5v$

64. $4n^2 = 6n + 10$

69. $2a^2 - a = 21$

65. $5r^2 - 13 = 8r$

70. $n^2 = -6n - 5$

71. $2x^2 = 63 - 11x$

76. $3x^2 - x = 140$

72. $2n^2 + 10n = -12$

77. $4a^2 - 20 = 2a$

73. $4p^2 - 57 = -7p$

78. $x^2 - 12 = -x$

74. $n^2 = -3n + 88$

79. $3b^2 = 12b + 96$

75. $5n^2 + 7n = 34$

80. $2n^2 + 5 = 7n$

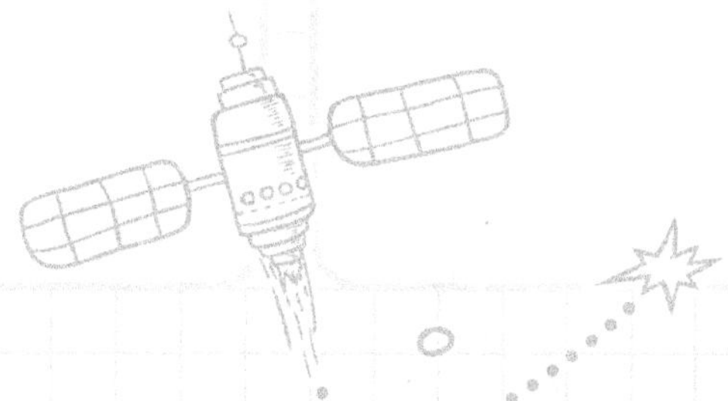

81. $5n^2 + n = 120$

82. $3v^2 - 112 = 10v$

83. $2p^2 + 9p = 18$

84. $6x^2 = 15 + x$

85. $5x^2 = 2x + 7$

86. $6a^2 + 3a = 108$

87. $2a^2 = -a + 120$

88. $5n^2 = 34 + 7n$

89. $n^2 + 7n = 98$

90. $3x^2 - 6 = -7x$

91. $b^2 + 4b = 21$

96. $6n^2 - 21 = 11n$

92. $5v^2 - 11v = 114$

97. $5a^2 = 7a + 90$

93. $p^2 - 3p = 130$

98. $n^2 + 4n = 32$

94. $n^2 - 6 = n$

99. $r^2 + 4r = 96$

95. $5b^2 - 11b = 12$

100. $3x^2 - 4x = 95$

Systems of linear equations are a set of two or more equations that contain two or more variables. The solution to a system of linear equations is the set of values for each variable that makes all the equations in the system true. In this chapter, we will discuss the methods used to solve systems of linear equations by the substitution method or the elimination method.

The **Substitution Method** involves solving one equation for one variable in terms of the other variable, and then substituting the expression into the other equation to eliminate one variable. The steps to solve a system of linear equations by substitution are as follows:

Step 1: Solve one equation for one variable in terms of the other variable.

Step 2: Substitute the expression into the other equation to eliminate one variable.

Step 3: Solve for the remaining variable.

Step 4: Substitute the value of the remaining variable into one of the original equations to find the value of the other variable.

Step 5: Check that the values satisfy both equations.

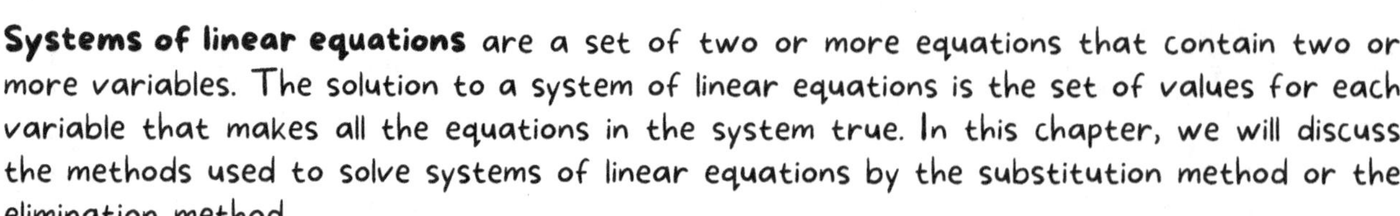

Guided Practice Question #1:

$2x + 3y = 7$
$x - y = 1$

Step 1: Solve one of the equations for one of the variables.
We can solve the second equation for x by adding y to both sides:

$x - y = 1$
$x = y + 1$

Step 2: Substitute the expression obtained in Step 1 into the other equation.
We can substitute $y + 1$ for x in the first equation:

$2x + 3y = 7$
$2(y + 1) + 3y = 7$

Step 3: Solve for the remaining variable.
Simplifying the equation obtained in Step **2** gives:

$2y + 2 + 3y = 7$

$5y + 2 = 7$

$5y = 5$

$y = 1$

Step 4: Substitute the value obtained in Step **3** into one of the original equations to solve for the other variable.
We can substitute $y = 1$ into the second equation to solve for x:

$x - y = 1$

$x - 1 = 1$

$x = 2$

Step 5: Check the solution by substituting the values obtained in Steps **3** and **4** into one of the original equations.
We can substitute $x = 2$ and $y = 1$ into one of the two original equations to verify that the solution is correct:

$2x + 3y = 7$

$2(2) + 3(1) = 7$

$4 + 3 = 7$ **CORRECT**

Therefore, the solution to the system of linear equations is $x = 2$, $y = 1$. We can write the answer also in **(x,y)** coordinate form which is **(2,1)**.

Guided Practice Question #2:

$$3x + 4y = -5$$
$$2x - 3y = 8$$

Let's solve for x in the second equation.

$$2x - 3y = 8$$
$$2x = 3y + 8$$
$$x = \frac{3}{2}y + 4$$

Now, we will substitute this x value for the x in the first equation.

$$3x + 4y = -5$$
$$3\left(\frac{3}{2}y + 4\right) + 4y = -5$$

Let's go ahead and solve.

$$\frac{9}{2}y + 4 + 12 + 4y = -5$$
$$\frac{17}{2}y = -17$$
$$y = -2$$

We know that $y = -2$ so we can plug that into either of the two original equations to figure out what x is.

$$2x - 3(-2) = 8$$
$$2x + 6 = 8$$
$$2x = 2$$
$$x = 1$$

The solution is $x = 1$ and $y = -2$. You can double-check the solution by plugging these variables back into one of the original equations. We can write the answer also in (x, y) coordinate form which is $(1, -2)$.

We can solve systems of linear equations using another method called **Elimination Method**. This method involves adding or subtracting the equations to eliminate one variable and solve for the other.

The general idea of the elimination method is to manipulate the equations so that one variable has opposite coefficients in each equation, and then add or subtract the equations to eliminate that variable. This results in an equation in one variable, which can be solved to obtain the value of that variable. The value of the other variable can then be obtained by substituting the value obtained into one of the original equations.

Let's consider an example of a system of two linear equations:

$3x + 2y = 9$ (Equation 1)

$2x + 6y = 6$ (Equation 2)

Step 1: Choose a variable to eliminate. For this example, let's go ahead and eliminate the variable "x". How can we do this? We can manipulate Equation 1 by multiplying the entire equation by **-2** and we can multiply Equation 2 by **3**.

$$-2 \quad (3x + 2y = 9)$$
$$3 \quad (2x + 6y = 6)$$

That gives us

$$-6x - 4y = -18$$
$$+6x - 18y = 18$$

This is great because we just eliminated the variable x. We are just left with **-22**y = **0**. Let's solve for y, by dividing both side by **-22**.

$y = $ **0**.

Since we now know that y = **0**, we can plug that value into any of our original equations. Let's plug that into our original Equation 1.

$3x + 2(0) = 9$

$3x + 0 = 9$

$3x = 9$

$x = 3$

The solution is x = 3 and y = 0. You can double-check the solution by plugging these variables back into one of the original equations. We can write the answer also in (x,y) coordinate form which is (3,0).

Let's take a look at one more practice example using the Elimination Method.

$-x + 5y = 8$

$3x + 7y = -2$

We can easily get rid of the variable x if we manipulate Equation 1 by multiplying by **3** and then adding the two equations together.

$$\begin{cases} -x + 5y = 8 \\ 3x + 7y = -2 \end{cases} \xrightarrow{\times 3} \begin{cases} -3x + 15y = 24 \\ 3x + 7y = -2 \end{cases}$$

$$\begin{array}{r} -3x + 15y = 24 \\ + \quad 3x + 7y = -2 \\ \hline 22y = 22 \\ \dfrac{22y}{22} = \dfrac{22}{22} \\ y = 1 \end{array}$$

We know $y=1$ so let's plug that back into one of the original equations and solve for x.

$-x + 5(1) = 8$

$-x + 5 = 8$

$-x = 3$

$x = -3$

The solution is $x = -3$ and $y = 1$. You can double-check the solution by plugging these variables back into one of the original equations. We can write the answer also in (x,y) coordinate form which is $(-3,1)$.

Try the following practice questions using either the **Substitution Method or the Elimination Method.**

Solve the system of equations using the Substitution Method or the Elimination Method.

Solve the system of equations using the Substitution Method or the Elimination Method.

1. $x + y = 1$
   $4x - 3y = -24$

2. $3x - 2y = 16$
   $x + y = 2$

3. $2x - 9y = -18$
   $4x - 3y = 24$

4. $4x - 3y = 3$
   $x - 3y = 12$

5. $x - 2y = -4$
   $11x - 4y = 28$

6. $2x - 3y = -12$
   $2x - y = -8$

7. $5x + 9y = -9$
   $x - 3y = 27$

8. $7x + 2y = -18$
   $x - 2y = 2$

9. $2x - y = -7$
   $4x + y = 1$

13. $x + y = -7$
    $3x - 5y = -5$

10. $x = -5$
    $8x - 5y = -25$

14. $x + y = 4$
    $3x - y = 4$

11. $9x - 2y = -6$
    $x - y = 4$

15. $4x + y = -2$
    $x + y = -5$

12. $x + 3y = -15$
    $10x + 9y = 18$

16. $x - 9y = 45$
    $x + y = 5$

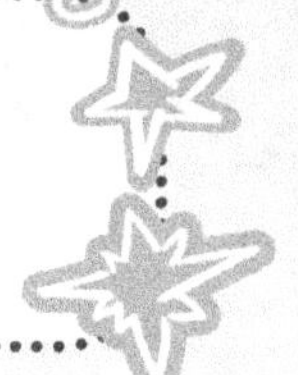

17. $2x - 3y = 12$
$13x - 3y = -21$

21. $x + 2y = -4$
$4x + y = 5$

18. $5x + 3y = 18$
$x + 6y = -18$

22. $4x + 9y = 9$
$2x - 9y = 45$

19. $17x + 8y = 72$
$3x + 8y = -40$

23. $13x - y = -8$
$x + y = -6$

20. $5x + 3y = 9$
$x - 3y = 9$

24. $3x + 5y = 30$
$2x - 5y = -5$

25. $8x + 3y = -27$
$7x - 3y = -18$

29. $x + 4y = 24$
$13x - 4y = 32$

26. $x + y = -5$
$15x + 4y = 24$

30. $x + 3y = -9$
$3x + 2y = 8$

27. $4x - 7y = -14$
$13x - 7y = 49$

31. $x + 7y = 49$
$10x + 7y = -14$

28. $x + 4y = 4$
$3x + 2y = -8$

32. $7x + 4y = 20$
$x + 2y = -10$

33. $5x - 4y = 16$
$x + 4y = 32$

37. $5x - 3y = 24$
$7x + 6y = 54$

34. $4x + y = 7$
$2x - y = 5$

38. $7x - y = 6$
$y = 1$

35. $x - 5y = -35$
$x - y = -3$

39. $10x + 9y = -36$
$x - 9y = -63$

36. $8x + 3y = 24$
$x + 3y = -18$

40. $x + 2y = 8$
$11x - 2y = 16$

41. $x - 3y = -15$
$11x + 9y = -81$

45. $x - 3y = -3$
$3x - 2y = -16$

42. $2x + 5y = -40$
$8x - 5y = -10$

46. $2x - 7y = -7$
$3x + 7y = -28$

43. $5x + 8y = 72$
$5x - 8y = 8$

47. $2x - y = -2$
$3x + y = 7$

44. $9x + 7y = 49$
$5x - 7y = 49$

48. $x + 6y = -12$
$x = 6$

49. $2x + y = -7$
$9x - y = -4$

50. $2x - y = 4$
$11x + y = 9$

51. $x + y = -3$
$x - y = 5$

52. $x + 4y = -4$
$7x - 8y = -64$

53. $x + 5y = -45$
$6x - 5y = 10$

54. $16x + 3y = -24$
$x + 3y = 21$

55. $x + 4y = -32$
$x + y = -5$

56. $x + 7y = -56$
$15x + 7y = 42$

57. $2x - 3y = 15$
$x + 3y = 12$

61. $x + 2y = 4$
$5x + 3y = -15$

58. $4x + 3y = -27$
$x + 9y = 18$

62. $x - 3y = -3$
$2x - y = 9$

59. $6x - y = 4$
$x + 2y = 18$

63. $7x - 4y = 8$
$x - 4y = -16$

60. $2x - 3y = 12$
$5x + 3y = 9$

64. $9x + 8y = -24$
$x + 8y = 40$

65. $9x + y = -1$
$x + y = 7$

69. $8x - 3y = -24$
$2x - 3y = 12$

66. $x - 6y = 30$
$11x - 6y = -30$

70. $x - 3y = 15$
$13x - 6y = -36$

67. $13x + 8y = -48$
$x + 4y = 20$

71. $x - y = 6$
$y = -5$

68. $5x + 2y = -2$
$y = 9$

72. $11x + y = 9$
$x - y = 3$

73. $5x - 8y = -64$
$5x + 4y = -28$

77. $2x - 3y = 3$
$3x - y = -6$

74. $5x - 9y = 36$
$16x - 9y = -63$

78. $8x - 9y = 27$
$x - 9y = -36$

75. $3x - y = 1$
$3x + y = 5$

79. $4x - 3y = -9$
$x - 9y = 72$

76. $3x + y = 1$
$3x - y = -7$

80. $x - 4y = -12$
$5x + 4y = -12$

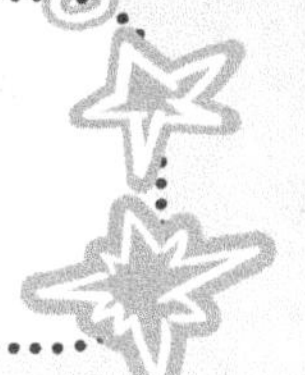

81. $x + y = -3$
$x - y = 9$

85. $16x + 9y = 81$
$x + 9y = -54$

82. $16x - 7y = 63$
$3x - 7y = -28$

86. $x - y = 7$
$2x + y = -4$

83. $5x - 3y = 12$
$4x + 3y = 15$

87. $2x + 5y = -5$
$8x - 5y = -45$

84. $x - 5y = 45$
$6x + 5y = -10$

88. $13x + y = -9$
$2x - y = -6$

89. $x - 7y = 14$
$4x + 7y = -49$

90. $14x + 5y = 35$
$x + 5y = -30$

91. $3x - 4y = -20$
$13x - 4y = 20$

92. $7x + y = 9$
$x - y = -1$

93. $2x + y = -4$
$8x - y = -6$

94. $x + y = 2$
$2x + 7y = -21$

95. $3x - y = 3$
$x - 2y = -14$

96. $6x + 7y = 14$
$x + 7y = -21$

97. $10x + 9y = 45$
    $2x - 9y = 63$

98. $x - 3y = -9$
    $7x - 6y = 12$

99. $7x - 2y = 10$
    $3x + 2y = 10$

100. $3x + 8y = -48$
    $2x + y = 7$

101. $3x - 4y = -20$
    $4x - y = 8$

102. $x + 4y = 20$
    $9x - 4y = 20$

103. $7x + 9y = 18$
    $x = 9$

104. $18x + 5y = -45$
    $4x + 5y = 25$

105. $x = -8$
$5x + 8y = 32$

109. $2x + 9y = -54$
$x - 3y = 3$

106. $x + 6y = 18$
$3x - 2y = 14$

110. $11x + y = -3$
$y = 8$

107. $3x - 4y = -32$
$7x + 2y = -18$

111. $4x + y = 5$
$x + y = 8$

108. $3x - y = -3$
$3x + y = 9$

112. $x + y = 3$
$3x - y = -7$

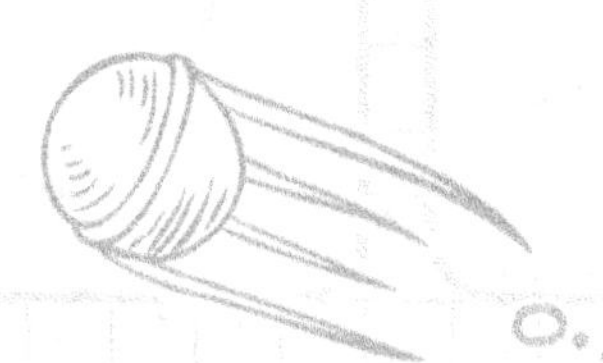

113. $x + y = -7$
$13x + y = 5$

117. $x - 2y = -6$
$x + 3y = 24$

114. $7x - 8y = 64$
$9x + 8y = 64$

118. $4x + y = -2$
$x - y = -3$

115. $4x + 5y = 35$
$11x - 5y = 40$

119. $4x + y = -5$
$2x - 3y = -27$

116. $x = 8$
$7x + 4y = 28$

120. $x - 3y = -27$
$11x + 3y = -9$

121. $x + 6y = 48$
$3x + y = -9$

125. $x - 2y = -2$
$2x - y = 2$

122. $14x - y = 9$
$x + y = 6$

126. $3x - 5y = -30$
$16x - 5y = 35$

123. $5x - 7y = 21$
$3x + 7y = 35$

127. $2x + 7y = 56$
$2x - y = 8$

124. $x + y = -3$
$x - 3y = -27$

128. $9x - 2y = 4$
$y = 7$

129. $3x - 2y = 6$
$x - 3y = -12$

133. $2x - 5y = -30$
$3x + 5y = 5$

130. $x = -7$
$5x - 7y = -28$

134. $3x - 2y = 16$
$x + 2y = 8$

131. $2x + y = -3$
$9x - y = -8$

135. $x = 4$
$7x + 4y = 12$

132. $x - y = -4$
$10x + 3y = -27$

136. $8x + 3y = 3$
$x + 3y = -18$

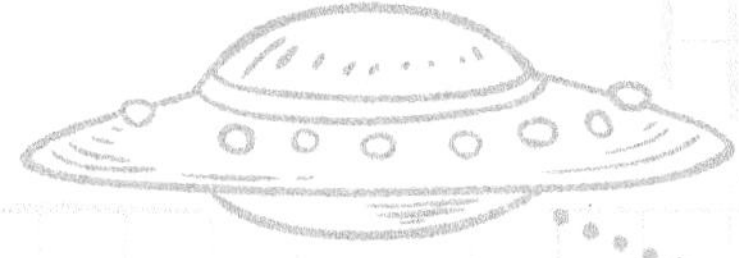

137. $8x - 3y = 18$
$5x + 3y = 21$

141. $x + 2y = 4$
$7x + 4y = -12$

138. $x - y = 5$
$7x + 6y = 48$

142. $x + y = 2$
$8x + y = -5$

139. $2x - 5y = 5$
$9x - 5y = 40$

143. $x + y = 3$
$6x - y = 4$

140. $x + 3y = 18$
$7x - 6y = 18$

144. $3x - y = -2$
$3x + y = 8$

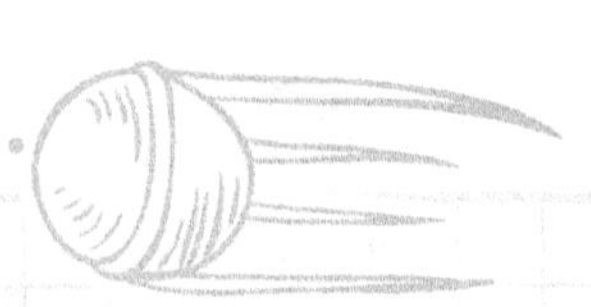

145. $7x - 9y = 72$
$7x + 9y = 54$

146. $3x + 2y = 2$
$x = 6$

147. $x - 3y = 15$
$10x - 3y = -12$

148. $5x - 2y = 18$
$2x - 3y = -6$

149. $x - 2y = 10$
$2x + 3y = 6$

150. $4x + y = -3$
$2x - y = -3$

151. $17x + 9y = -81$
$x + 9y = 63$

152. $x = -8$
$3x - 8y = -32$

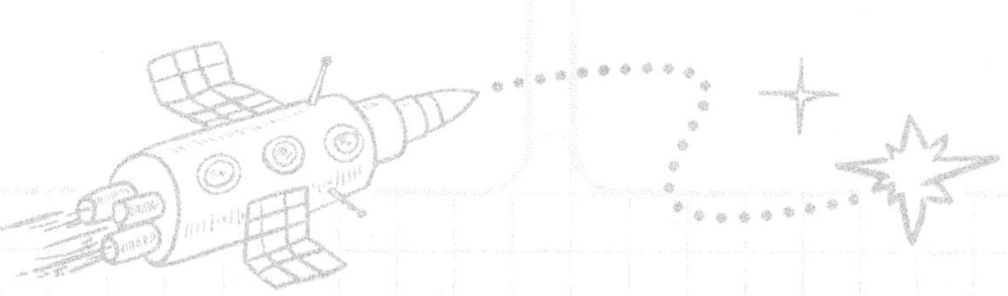

153. $x - 8y = 48$
$5x + 4y = 20$

157. $y = -2$
$7x - 5y = -25$

154. $x - 3y = 12$
$10x + 9y = 81$

158. $4x + 9y = 27$
$x - 3y = 12$

155. $3x + 4y = -12$
$3x - 4y = 36$

159. $x - 3y = 6$
$x + 3y = -24$

156. $x + y = -3$
$x - 3y = 21$

160. $12x + 7y = 63$
$y = -3$

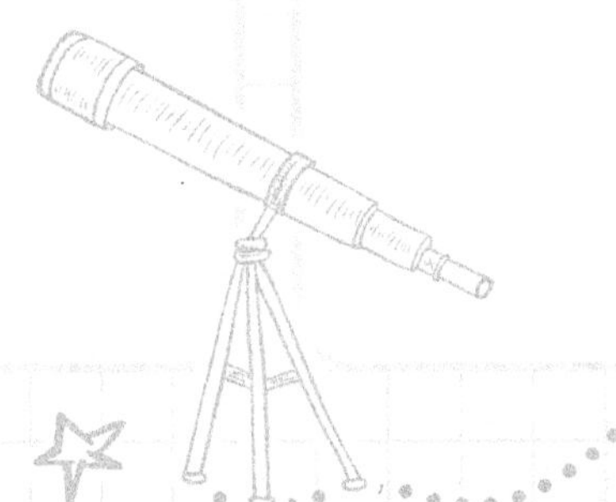

161. $3x + y = 1$
$2x - y = 4$

162. $x + y = -5$
$3x - y = -7$

163. $4x - 3y = 18$
$2x - 9y = -36$

164. $x - y = -2$
$3x + 8y = -72$

165. $2x - 3y = -6$
$11x - 3y = 21$

166. $14x - 5y = 30$
$2x - 5y = -30$

167. $x + y = -9$
$3x - y = -3$

168. $x - y = 9$
$7x + 3y = 3$

169. $x = 8$
     $x - y = 9$

170. $3x - 5y = -25$
     $16x - 5y = 40$

171. $11x + 7y = -49$
     $x + 7y = 21$

172. $11x + 5y = 35$
     $4x - 5y = 40$

173. $6x - y = 3$
     $x - y = -7$

174. $3x + 2y = -12$
     $5x - y = -7$

175. $6x - y = 1$
     $x - y = -4$

176. $x - y = -4$
     $5x - y = 8$

177. $9x - 4y = 12$
$x - 2y = -8$

181. $5x - 3y = -21$
$x = -6$

178. $2x - 3y = 27$
$11x + 9y = 72$

182. $7x + 9y = 72$
$x - 3y = 6$

179. $y = 2$
$5x - 2y = -14$

183. $x + 2y = -14$
$3x + y = 3$

180. $4x + 3y = -27$
$11x - 3y = -18$

184. $4x + 5y = -15$
$14x + 5y = 35$

185. $3x + 4y = 16$
     $x - 2y = 2$

189. $7x - 6y = 6$
     $x - 6y = 42$

186. $2x - 3y = -18$
     $14x - 3y = 18$

190. $x - 3y = 12$
     $7x + 3y = 12$

187. $2x + 9y = 63$
     $10x - 9y = 45$

191. $9x + 4y = -32$
     $5x - 4y = -24$

188. $3x - 8y = 64$
     $7x + 4y = 36$

192. $5x - 7y = -42$
     $9x + 7y = -56$

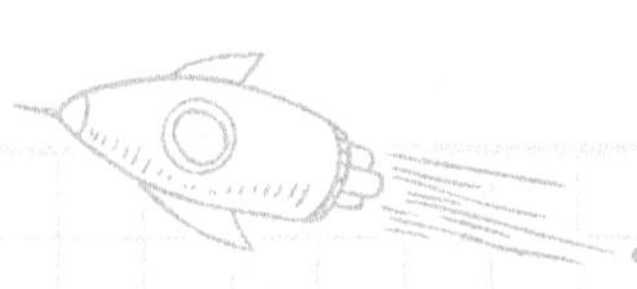

193. $11x + 8y = -16$
$3x + 8y = 48$

197. $3x + 2y = 12$
$x - 4y = 32$

194. $2x - y = -9$
$x - 9y = 72$

198. $x - y = 7$
$x + y = 1$

195. $7x - 3y = -15$
$x - 2y = 12$

199. $3x - 4y = -12$
$7x - 2y = 16$

196. $x + 2y = 4$
$5x - 2y = -16$

200. $8x - 7y = 49$
$2x + 7y = 21$

201. $3x - 2y = 10$
$3x + 2y = 2$

205. $x + 8y = -72$
$x - 2y = 8$

202. $11x + 8y = -24$
$x - 8y = -72$

206. $3x + 4y = -20$
$3x - 2y = -8$

203. $x = -7$
$4x + 7y = 35$

207. $3x + 5y = -25$
$x - 5y = 5$

204. $8x - 5y = -5$
$x + 5y = -40$

208. $11x - 4y = 16$
$x + 4y = 32$

209. $x - 7y = 49$
$\quad\quad x - y = 1$

213. $13x + 3y = 24$
$\quad\quad 2x + 3y = -9$

210. $x + y = 7$
$\quad\quad 13x - 2y = 16$

214. $6x + y = 6$
$\quad\quad x + y = -4$

211. $x + 9y = -54$
$\quad\quad 14x + 9y = 63$

215. $10x + 3y = 24$
$\quad\quad x + 3y = -3$

212. $x - 3y = 18$
$\quad\quad 11x - 3y = -12$

216. $7x + 3y = 12$
$\quad\quad 4x - 3y = 21$

217. $y = -7$
$13x + y = 6$

218. $2x - y = 2$
$x - 4y = -20$

219. $11x - 6y = -48$
$5x + 6y = -48$

220. $11x - y = 4$
$x - y = -6$

221. $x + 2y = 18$
$2x - y = -4$

222. $13x - 9y = -81$
$2x - 9y = 18$

223. $7x - 4y = 24$
$x + y = 5$

224. $17x + y = -9$
$x + y = 7$

225. $4x - 3y = 27$
$\quad\quad y = -5$

229. $2x + y = 6$
$\quad\quad 5x - y = 1$

226. $4x + y = 9$
$\quad\quad x + y = 3$

230. $x - 2y = -8$
$\quad\quad 7x + 6y = -36$

227. $x - y = 8$
$\quad\quad 11x + 2y = 10$

231. $6x + y = -7$
$\quad\quad x + y = -2$

228. $x = -2$
$\quad\quad x - 2y = -8$

232. $x - 2y = 4$
$\quad\quad x + 8y = 24$

233. $13x - 9y = 63$
$x = 9$

237. $10x - 3y = 9$
$x + 3y = 24$

234. $x + 2y = -8$
$4x + y = 3$

238. $x - 2y = -4$
$9x + 2y = -16$

235. $x + 4y = -4$
$11x + 4y = 36$

239. $6x - 7y = -35$
$4x + 7y = -35$

236. $2x + 3y = -24$
$x - 2y = 2$

240. $x + y = 8$
$7x - 2y = 2$

241. $6x + y = 3$
$y = 9$

245. $2x + y = 6$
$y = -4$

242. $16x - 7y = 56$
$2x - 7y = -42$

246. $x + 6y = -42$
$7x - 3y = -24$

243. $5x - 4y = 8$
$x + 8y = 72$

247. $x - 9y = 9$
$7x - 9y = -45$

244. $2x - 7y = -63$
$9x + 7y = -14$

248. $y = -9$
$5x - 3y = 12$

249. $9x - 4y = 8$
$x - 4y = -24$

253. $7x - 2y = 10$
$3x - 4y = -24$

250. $4x + 3y = 3$
$x + 3y = -15$

254. $4x - 3y = -9$
$x + 3y = -6$

251. $x + 2y = 10$
$x = -8$

255. $9x + 5y = 35$
$x - 5y = 15$

252. $x = -5$
$8x - 5y = -20$

256. $2x - y = -5$
$x - 2y = -4$

257. $7x - 8y = -16$
$x - 8y = -64$

261. $x - y = 5$
$4x - y = 2$

258. $11x - 2y = -18$
$3x + 2y = -10$

262. $17x + 8y = -64$
$3x + 8y = 48$

259. $6x - y = 9$
$x + y = 5$

263. $11x - 7y = -63$
$3x + 7y = -35$

260. $5x - 6y = 36$
$7x + 6y = 36$

264. $3x - 4y = 36$
$x + y = 5$

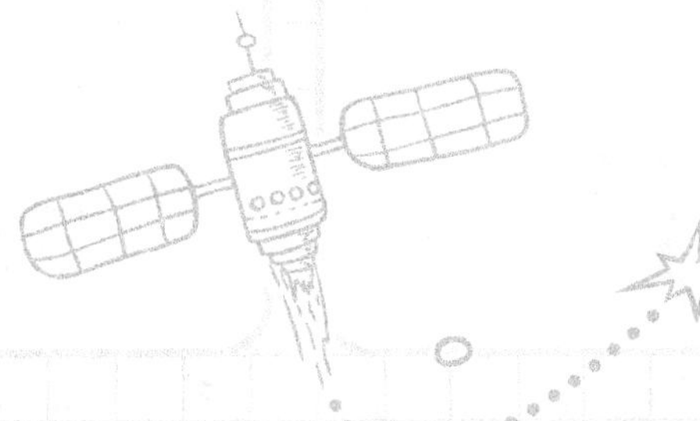

265. $x - 2y = -16$
$15x - 2y = 12$

269. $11x + y = -2$
$x + y = 8$

266. $2x + 5y = -15$
$x - 5y = 30$

270. $2x + 3y = 3$
$10x + 3y = -21$

267. $2x + 7y = -49$
$8x + 7y = -7$

271. $3x - y = 7$
$7x + 3y = 27$

268. $y = 9$
$5x - 3y = -12$

272. $x + 6y = 24$
$2x + y = -7$

273. $5x - 2y = -14$
$2x + y = -2$

277. $6x + 7y = 35$
$5x - 7y = 42$

274. $13x + 4y = -36$
$x - 4y = -20$

278. $x + 2y = 16$
$7x + y = -5$

275. $16x - 3y = -24$
$x - y = 5$

279. $7x + 9y = -36$
$x - 9y = -36$

276. $7x - 2y = -2$
$x + 2y = 18$

280. $3x - 8y = 48$
$x + 2y = 2$

281. $2x - 3y = -21$
$8x + 9y = -63$

285. $x - 9y = 63$
$x + y = 3$

282. $7x - 8y = 48$
$3x + 4y = 28$

286. $14x - 5y = 40$
$x - 5y = -25$

283. $x + 2y = -12$
$5x - 6y = -12$

287. $y = -2$
$x - y = -4$

284. $x - 9y = 72$
$2x - y = -9$

288. $3x - 4y = -24$
$3x - y = 3$

289. $7x - 3y = 15$
$x - 3y = -3$

293. $4x - 7y = 56$
$13x + 7y = 63$

290. $7x - 6y = -30$
$x + 6y = -18$

294. $x - y = -7$
$2x + 3y = -9$

291. $x = -5$
$3x + 5y = -30$

295. $3x + y = -1$
$4x - y = 8$

292. $x + y = 5$
$8x + y = -9$

296. $y = -8$
$7x + 6y = -6$

Answer
(x+c)(x-c)=x²-c²
16

BRAIN
HUNTER

Chapter 1: Algebraic Expressions

Part A: Evaluating Expressions

#	Ans	#	Ans	#	Ans	#	Ans	#	Ans	#	Ans	#	Ans	#	Ans	#	Ans	#	Ans
1.	-7	10.	15	19.	-4	28.	14	37.	2	46.	9	55.	6	64.	4	73.	42	82.	-9
2.	4	11.	-6	20.	-7	29.	100	38.	-99	47.	17	56.	80	65.	-2	74.	57	83.	2
3.	-61	12.	56	21.	14	30.	9	39.	-26	48.	19	57.	-29	66.	64	75.	4	84.	81
4.	-14	13.	90	22.	-3	31.	2	40.	-81	49.	12	58.	-38	67.	-35	76.	8	85.	-17
5.	-16	14.	2	23.	6	32.	80	41.	45	50.	15	59.	-32	68.	21	77.	59	86.	33
6.	26	15.	5	24.	-2	33.	-30	42.	1	51.	-9	60.	-24	69.	6	78.	17	87.	-10
7.	-3	16.	-58	25.	-6	34.	2	43.	12	52.	72	61.	2	70.	-17	79.	5	88.	56
8.	-2	17.	8	26.	1	35.	-7	44.	48	53.	-28	62.	-10	71.	5	80.	-2	89.	23
9.	21	18.	33	27.	9	36.	-32	45.	85	54.	-81	63.	-8	72.	-11	81.	91	90.	18

Chapter 1: Algebraic Expressions

Part B. Solving linear algebraic equations

#	Ans	#	Ans	#	Ans	#	Ans	#	Ans	#	Ans	#	Ans	#	Ans	#	Ans	#	Ans
1.	{7}	18.	{9}	36.	{8}	54.	{-7}	72.	{3}	90.	{2}	108.	{11}	126.	{20}	144.	{18}	162.	{-289}
2.	{-5}	19.	{6}	37.	{10}	55.	{0}	73.	{5}	91.	{8}	109.	{-3}	127.	{-200}	145.	{-27}	163.	{-27}
3.	{-4}	20.	{-1}	38.	{1}	56.	{-6}	74.	{-6}	92.	{16}	110.	{1}	128.	{-10}	146.	{-19}	164.	{-330}
4.	{-6}	21.	{4}	39.	{-6}	57.	{6}	75.	{1}	93.	{-16}	111.	{-3}	129.	{-11}	147.	{-11}	165.	{-28}
5.	{-1}	22.	{9}	40.	{-9}	58.	{10}	76.	{7}	94.	{-4}	112.	{13}	130.	{84}	148.	{-6}	166.	{-408}
6.	{1}	23.	{6}	41.	{7}	59.	{5}	77.	{-8}	95.	{-3}	113.	{20}	131.	{4}	149.	{13}	167.	{17}
7.	{0}	24.	{-3}	42.	{-7}	60.	{-1}	78.	{-10}	96.	{-29}	114.	{-5}	132.	{4}	150.	{-39}	168.	{-207}
8.	{3}	25.	{-4}	43.	{6}	61.	{0}	79.	{-2}	97.	{11}	115.	{-18}	133.	{9}	151.	{-8}	169.	{-8}
9.	{8}	26.	{10}	44.	{1}	62.	{5}	80.	{-9}	98.	{-2}	116.	{-27}	134.	{-29}	152.	{-315}	170.	{-19}
10.	{1}	27.	{-8}	45.	{-4}	63.	{9}	81.	{-4}	99.	{-20}	117.	{6}	135.	{-182}	153.	{-17}	171.	{12}
11.	{3}	28.	{2}	46.	{7}	64.	{8}	82.	{-9}	100.	{15}	118.	{231}	136.	{-26}	154.	{17}	172.	{27}
12.	{7}	29.	{1}	47.	{1}	65.	{-5}	83.	{-8}	101.	{522}	119.	{-29}	137.	{260}	155.	{-2}	173.	{95}
13.	{-4}	30.	{-1}	48.	{6}	66.	{-9}	84.	{-4}	102.	{4}	120.	{-198}	138.	{21}	156.	{-27}	174.	{11}
14.	{-8}	31.	{-5}	49.	{0}	67.	{-4}	85.	{2}	103.	{5}	121.	{19}	139.	{25}	157.	{182}	175.	{-29}
15.	{3}	32.	{0}	50.	{2}	68.	{3}	86.	{10}	104.	{-17}	122.	{-609}	140.	{20}	158.	{-50}	176.	{-24}
16.	{-6}	33.	{-8}	51.	{-5}	69.	{1}	87.	{5}	105.	{10}	123.	{26}	141.	{-754}	159.	{24}	177.	{-200}
17.	{-6}	34.	{5}	52.	{4}	70.	{2}	88.	{-4}	106.	{4}	124.	{22}	142.	{-1}	160.	{14}	178.	{4}
		35.	{-7}	53.	{-3}	71.	{10}	89.	{-5}	107.	{-11}	125.	{-200}	143.	{4}	161.	{-19}	179.	{27}
																		180.	{621}

Chapter 2: Scientific Notation

1. 3.721×10^{-5}
2. 6.561×10^{15}
3. 2.55×10^{5}
4. 2.804×10^{10}
5. 2.972×10^{7}
6. 9.113×10^{-8}
7. 1.681×10^{-7}
8. 4.361×10^{10}
9. 3×10^{2}
10. 7.256×10^{4}
11. 4×10^{-6}
12. 4.62×10^{1}
13. 5.36×10^{1}
14. 1.177×10^{5}
15. 1.25×10^{1}
16. 2.915×10^{4}
17. 1.005×10^{6}
18. 5.476×10^{-3}
19. 4.306×10^{-7}
20. 4.588×10^{-1}
21. 2.275×10^{8}
22. 3.672×10^{5}
23. 5.22×10^{10}
24. 2.271×10^{-1}
25. 4.429×10^{-2}
26. 4.23×10^{8}
27. 1.321×10^{9}
28. 7.92×10^{0}
29. 9.259×10^{1}
30. 9.14×10^{5}
31. 6.918×10^{-1}
32. 7.407×10^{2}
33. 2.369×10^{5}
34. 6.897×10^{1}
35. 1.5×10^{-3}
36. 3.315×10^{-5}
37. 3.087×10^{5}
38. 1.893×10^{6}
39. 3.022×10^{-3}
40. 9.308×10^{4}
41. 2.605×10^{6}
42. 2.16×10^{-7}
43. 1.384×10^{-5}
44. 4.666×10^{16}
45. 7.74×10^{5}
46. 3.029×10^{6}
47. 1.272×10^{5}
48. 5.143×10^{-1}
49. 1.801×10^{-11}
50. 9.429×10^{3}
51. 1.531×10^{-1}
52. 4.444×10
53. 2.52×10^{8}
54. 1.053×10^{-2}
55. 8.722×10^{7}
56. 5.926×10^{-1}
57. 3.92×10^{5}
58. 3.077×10^{-4}
59. 3.45×10^{-2}
60. 5.688×10^{8}
61. 8.154×10^{1}
62. 4.918×10^{7}
63. 4.025×10^{8}
64. 2.83×10^{13}
65. 9.303×10^{-1}
66. 1.469×10^{12}
67. 8.759×10^{-3}
68. 2.52×10^{-9}
69. 1.569×10^{3}
70. 3.579×10^{20}
71. 1.002×10^{-2}
72. 2.5×10^{9}
73. 1.86×10^{-6}
74. 8.88×10^{-12}
75. 4.091×10^{5}
76. 1.8×10^{11}
77. 2.233×10^{2}
78. 4.929×10^{7}
79. 2.16×10^{-6}
80. 3.844×10^{-3}
81. 5.6×10^{3}
82. 1.573×10^{11}
83. 1.877×10^{-9}
84. 6.829×10^{-2}
85. 1.184×10^{-5}
86. 2.067×10^{3}
87. 1.127×10^{7}
88. 6.966×10^{2}
89. 1.291×10^{-9}
90. 1.48×10^{-4}
91. 6.667×10^{5}
92. 4.487×10^{-3}
93. 9.8×10^{-10}
94. 7.407×10^{-1}
95. 8.899×10^{7}
96. 7.776×10^{-2}
97. 2.116×10^{-1}
98. 4.288×10^{1}
99. 1.774×10^{1}
100. 3.64×10^{-2}
101. 4.084×10^{16}
102. 1.38×10^{-1}
103. 1.104×10^{7}
104. 1.224×10^{-2}
105. 7.085×10^{-1}
106. 2.586×10^{11}
107. 1.352×10^{-4}
108. 9.88×10^{-10}
109. 1.955×10^{4}
110. 1.024×10^{1}
111. 2.646×10^{13}
112. 1.612×10^{0}
113. 9.27×10^{-1}
114. 9.492×10^{-3}
115. 8.94×10^{1}
116. 7.5×10^{-7}
117. 3.682×10^{-2}
118. 9.556×10^{-11}
119. 3.24×10^{6}
120. 4.02×10^{2}
121. 6.099×10^{2}
122. 9.25×10^{0}
123. 5.13×10^{0}
124. 8.085×10^{8}
125. 1.072×10^{0}
126. 4.55×10^{-4}
127. 2.16×10^{14}
128. 2.092×10^{5}
129. 6.561×10^{-6}
130. 3.618×10^{4}
131. 7.744×10^{-5}
132. 1.426×10^{-7}
133. 2.623×10^{8}
134. 2.889×10^{-1}
135. 1.066×10^{-8}
136. 6.76×10^{4}
137. 2.797×10^{-9}
138. 2.302×10^{4}
139. 4.436×10^{1}
140. 2.56×10^{8}
141. 3.792×10^{-8}
142. 1.418×10^{11}
143. 6.667×10^{7}
144. 7.053×10^{-11}
145. 7.497×10^{9}
146. 1.92×10^{7}
147. 5.376×10^{4}
148. 1.542×10^{-2}
149. 6.09×10^{-6}
150. 2.4×10^{-9}
151. 1.1×10^{1}
152. 5.333×10^{-2}
153. 1.72×10^{4}
154. 1.82×10^{1}
155. 1.179×10^{9}
156. 9.263×10^{2}
157. 2.516×10^{-1}
158. 1.813×10^{9}
159. 5.769×10^{4}
160. 2.538×10^{-3}
161. 1.852×10^{8}
162. 8.889×10^{1}
163. 3.921×10^{-1}
164. 5.175×10^{4}
165. 7.662×10^{-1}
166. 4.39×10^{-5}
167. 9.618×10^{-4}
168. 1.104×10^{-1}
169. 8.111×10^{7}
170. 8.333×10^{5}
171. 3.067×10^{3}
172. 9.153×10^{-2}
173. 6.776×10^{-11}
174. 1.202×10^{2}
175. 1.025×10^{5}
176. 2.976×10^{-3}
177. 6.428×10^{2}
178. 1.68×10^{-2}
179. 1.233×10^{1}
180. 6×10^{1}
181. 5.41×10^{-1}
182. 5.418×10^{-4}
183. 1.704×10^{-1}
184. 1.173×10^{5}
185. 2.424×10^{-5}
186. 4.02×10^{-2}
187. 7.29×10^{-10}
188. 3.666×10^{-5}
189. 7.317×10^{-2}
190. 1.786×10^{-6}
191. 3.752×10^{2}
192. 5.72×10^{-3}
193. 1.557×10^{1}
194. 1.95×10^{-5}
195. 6.93×10^{3}
196. 1.804×10^{-4}
197. 9×10^{5}
198. 4.761×10^{-7}
199. 5.846×10^{-5}
200. 5.156×10^{5}
201. 3.16×10^{2}
202. 3.333×10^{-9}
203. 3.45×10^{-7}

204. 1.347×10^9	236. 2.25×10^{-10}	268. 1.759×10^{-1}	300. 2.795×10^4	332. 1.892×10^{-3}
205. 5.58×10^1	237. 3.66×10^{12}	269. 2.704×10^{-11}	301. 6.908×10^{-1}	333. 3.2×10^8
206. 1.371×10^5	238. 2.16×10^8	270. 7.616×10^1	302. 1.969×10^{-6}	334. 1.838×10^1
207. 2.56×10^{-10}	239. 2.22×10^{-5}	271. 3.692×10^6	303. 2.424×10^1	335. 2.43×10^7
208. 9.03×10^4	240. 4.2×10^{-6}	272. 1.333×10^{-5}	304. 2.097×10^9	336. 3.571×10^{-5}
209. 7.744×10^5	241. 1.646×10^{-2}	273. 8.226×10^3	305. 5.34×10^{-1}	337. 8.55×10^{-2}
210. 5.789×10^{24}	242. 2.479×10^5	274. 1.948×10^2	306. 2.765×10^2	338. 3.536×10^0
211. 1.8×10^{-1}	243. 5.47×10^{-8}	275. 7.416×10^5	307. 5.383×10^{10}	339. 1.151×10^{-3}
212. 5.6×10^{-5}	244. 9.897×10^2	276. 2.846×10^4	308. 3.581×10^{-11}	340. 7.26×10^{-5}
213. 1.196×10^0	245. 9.325×10^{-11}	277. 6.6×10^{-1}	309. 5.52×10^{-4}	341. 9.603×10^5
214. 2.568×10^{-6}	246. 2.148×10^{-3}	278. 1.833×10^{-2}	310. 3.3×10^4	342. 3.78×10^{-3}
215. 3.185×10^0	247. 6×10^{-3}	279. 3.231×10^1	311. 1.856×10^{-1}	343. 8.14×10^{-1}
216. 1.686×10^5	248. 1.581×10^{-14}	280. 9.887×10^{34}	312. 1.414×10^{11}	344. 5.834×10^8
217. 3.797×10^{-13}	249. 1.563×10^{-26}	281. 3.08×10^7	313. 1.12×10^{11}	345. 1.96×10^{-2}
218. 3.083×10^{-6}	250. 7.527×10^6	282. 1.418×10^{-1}	314. 1.033×10^4	346. 3.3×10^{-1}
219. 5.556×10^{-8}	251. 5.957×10^{-9}	283. 1.242×10^2	315. 1.938×10^9	347. 6.365×10^0
220. 1.296×10^{11}	252. 1.312×10^6	284. 1.198×10^5	316. 7.6×10^{-8}	348. 3.76×10^{-1}
221. 6.656×10^8	253. 9.004×10^4	285. 2.857×10^{-1}	317. 1.217×10^4	349. 1.081×10^{-2}
222. 1.575×10^{11}	254. 4.851×10^4	286. 5.782×10^0	318. 1.529×10^0	350. 1.86×10^5
223. 2.75×10^{-1}	255. 9.459×10^1	287. 2.182×10^2	319. 2.2×10^2	351. 7.848×10^3
224. 2.743×10^{11}	256. 6.087×10^{-10}	288. 3.2×10^{-2}	320. 4.125×10^3	352. 9.96×10^{-3}
225. -4.982×10^1	257. 1.952×10^{-11}	289. 10×10^3	321. 1.792×10^1	353. 3.375×10^{-3}
226. 1.085×10^{-4}	258. 8.543×10^{-7}	290. 4.791×10^{15}	322. 2.53×10^2	354. 2.035×10^7
227. 8.82×10^{-3}	259. 1.043×10^6	291. 2.308×10^9	323. 2.383×10^{17}	355. 2.122×10^3
228. 4.32×10^9	260. 4×10^{-7}	292. 5.74×10^0	324. 2.978×10^8	356. 1.55×10^{-2}
229. 5.905×10^{29}	261. 4.667×10^{-2}	293. 2.345×10^2	325. 4.455×10^{-7}	357. 2.042×10^5
230. 1.068×10^{-2}	262. 3.478×10^{12}	294. 1.452×10^{10}	326. 1.386×10^{11}	358. 5.72×10^9
231. 4.68×10^2	263. 2.15×10^{-2}	295. 7.787×10^{-10}	327. 7.143×10^4	359. 3.438×10^8
232. 2.333×10^{-6}	264. 4.828×10^4	296. 6.586×10^2	328. 3.806×10^{-4}	360. 7.241×10^6
233. 8.316×10^6	265. 10×10^0	297. 5.429×10^{-9}	329. 1.35×10^4	
234. 1.98×10^4	266. 6.66×10^4	298. 1.92×10^{-5}	330. 5.327×10^{-3}	
235. 9.292×10^{-4}	267. 1.57×10^5	299. 8.226×10^{-1}	331. 4.8×10^{10}	

Chapter 3: Solving Absolute Value Equations

1. $\{20, -20\}$
2. $\{12, 4\}$
3. $\{10, -10\}$
4. $\{4, -4\}$
5. $\{6, -6\}$
6. $\{8, -8\}$
7. $\{25, -25\}$
8. $\{4, -10\}$
9. $\{8, 4\}$
10. $\{1, -11\}$
11. $\{-2, 2\}$
12. $\{4, -22\}$
13. $\{45, -45\}$
14. $\{16, 2\}$
15. $\{-10, 10\}$
16. $\{20, -8\}$
17. $\{28, -28\}$
18. $\{6, -6\}$
19. $\{-7, -13\}$
20. $\{13, 5\}$
21. $\{20, -20\}$
22. $\{5, -23\}$
23. $\{23, -5\}$
24. $\{10, -10\}$
25. $\{-7, 7\}$
26. $\{8, 4\}$
27. $\{5, -5\}$
28. $\{-1, 1\}$
29. $\{12, -12\}$
30. $\{10, -10\}$
31. $\left\{-2, -\dfrac{2}{3}\right\}$
32. $\left\{-\dfrac{59}{9}, 5\right\}$
33. $\left\{2, -\dfrac{26}{5}\right\}$
34. $\left\{-\dfrac{16}{3}, 8\right\}$
35. $\{18, 0\}$
36. $\left\{7, -\dfrac{21}{2}\right\}$
37. $\{-3, -9\}$
38. $\left\{\dfrac{62}{7}, -10\right\}$
39. $\left\{\dfrac{3}{2}, 1\right\}$
40. $\{-5, -9\}$
41. $\left\{-10, \dfrac{64}{5}\right\}$
42. $\left\{10, -\dfrac{26}{3}\right\}$
43. $\{2, -6\}$
44. $\left\{9, -\dfrac{53}{5}\right\}$
45. $\left\{7, -\dfrac{5}{3}\right\}$
46. $\{6, -8\}$
47. $\{-1, 2\}$
48. $\{7, -3\}$
49. $\left\{\dfrac{5}{2}, -2\right\}$
50. $\{3, 7\}$
51. $\left\{-6, \dfrac{11}{2}\right\}$
52. $\left\{\dfrac{47}{9}, -3\right\}$
53. $\left\{-\dfrac{17}{3}, 9\right\}$
54. $\{-10, 12\}$
55. $\left\{6, -\dfrac{38}{5}\right\}$
56. $\left\{4, -\dfrac{9}{2}\right\}$
57. $\left\{7, -\dfrac{17}{5}\right\}$
58. $\left\{3, -\dfrac{25}{7}\right\}$
59. $\left\{-6, -\dfrac{15}{2}\right\}$
60. $\{-2, 6\}$
61. $\left\{3, -\dfrac{5}{2}\right\}$
62. $\left\{7, -\dfrac{59}{9}\right\}$
63. $\{-4, 12\}$
64. $\left\{-1, -\dfrac{13}{5}\right\}$
65. $\{-1, -5\}$
66. $\left\{\dfrac{49}{9}, -5\right\}$
67. $\{2, 4\}$
68. $\left\{\dfrac{13}{2}, -4\right\}$
69. $\{10, -7\}$
70. $\left\{-\dfrac{37}{4}, 9\right\}$
71. $\left\{\dfrac{17}{10}, \dfrac{19}{10}\right\}$
72. $\{6, -10\}$
73. $\{0, 1\}$
74. $\left\{2, -\dfrac{3}{5}\right\}$
75. $\left\{\dfrac{17}{3}, -9\right\}$
76. $\left\{\dfrac{23}{5}, -1\right\}$
77. $\{0, 6\}$
78. $\left\{7, -\dfrac{42}{5}\right\}$
79. $\{4, -2\}$
80. $\left\{\dfrac{16}{9}, -2\right\}$
81. $\{-6, 4\}$
82. $\left\{-\dfrac{10}{3}, 4\right\}$
83. $\{5, -7\}$
84. $\{-20, 0\}$
85. $\left\{-\dfrac{61}{7}, 7\right\}$
86. $\left\{\dfrac{2}{9}, 2\right\}$
87. $\left\{2, -\dfrac{6}{5}\right\}$
88. $\left\{0, \dfrac{4}{9}\right\}$
89. $\{-2, 4\}$
90. $\{9, -11\}$
91. $\{2, -2\}$
92. $\{3, -3\}$
93. $\{4, -4\}$
94. $\{3, -3\}$
95. $\{6, -6\}$
96. $\{3, -3\}$
97. $\{6, -6\}$
98. $\{4, -4\}$
99. $\{1, -1\}$
100. $\{3, -3\}$
101. $\{5, -5\}$
102. $\{7, -7\}$
103. $\{8, -8\}$
104. $\{8, -8\}$
105. $\{9, -9\}$
106. $\{1, -1\}$
107. $\{1, -1\}$
108. $\{10, -10\}$
109. $\{4, -4\}$
110. $\{7, -7\}$
111. $\{7, -7\}$
112. $\{9, -9\}$
113. $\{5, -5\}$
114. $\{8, -8\}$
115. $\{3, -3\}$
116. $\{5, -5\}$
117. $\{4, -4\}$
118. $\{9, -9\}$
119. $\{7, -7\}$
120. $\{1, -1\}$
121. $\{4, -4\}$
122. $\{2, -2\}$
123. $\{2, -2\}$
124. $\{5, -5\}$
125. $\{8, -8\}$
126. $\{4, -4\}$
127. $\{9, -9\}$
128. $\{1, -1\}$
129. $\{7, -7\}$
130. $\{4, -4\}$
131. $\{8, -8\}$
132. $\{10, -10\}$
133. $\{3, -3\}$
134. $\{6, -6\}$
135. $\{4, -4\}$
136. $\{1, -1\}$
137. $\{6, -6\}$
138. $\{1, -1\}$
139. $\{10, -10\}$
140. $\{3, -3\}$
141. $\{10, -10\}$
142. $\{-8, 8\}$
143. $\{15, -9\}$
144. $\left\{-\dfrac{9}{4}, \dfrac{9}{4}\right\}$
145. $\left\{\dfrac{3}{2}, -\dfrac{3}{2}\right\}$
146. $\{29, -43\}$
147. $\{20, -28\}$
148. $\{6, -6\}$
149. $\{1, -1\}$
150. $\{17, 1\}$
151. $\{6, -6\}$
152. $\{-8, -10\}$
153. $\{6, -6\}$
154. $\{6, -6\}$
155. $\{-10, 10\}$
156. $\{13, -1\}$
157. $\{11, 3\}$
158. $\{6, -6\}$
159. $\{3, -3\}$
160. $\{31, -39\}$
161. $\{-3, 3\}$
162. $\{-3, 3\}$
163. $\{22, -4\}$
164. $\{6, -6\}$
165. $\{7, 5\}$
166. $\{29, -31\}$
167. $\{-5, -15\}$
168. $\{6, -14\}$
169. $\{17, 3\}$
170. $\{8, 0\}$
171. $\{30, -40\}$
172. $\{18, 0\}$
173. $\left\{-\dfrac{21}{2}, \dfrac{21}{2}\right\}$
174. $\{5, -17\}$
175. $\left\{-\dfrac{4}{3}, \dfrac{4}{3}\right\}$
176. $\{-1, 1\}$
177. $\{3, -3\}$
178. $\{-4, -16\}$
179. $\{19, 1\}$
180. $\{-1, -9\}$
181. $\{4, 2\}$
182. $\{22, -10\}$
183. $\{2, -2\}$
184. $\{10, -18\}$
185. $\{9, -11\}$
186. $\{9, -7\}$
187. $\{5, -3\}$
188. $\{3, -19\}$
189. $\{7, 1\}$
190. $\{-9, 9\}$
191. $\left\{\dfrac{106}{9}, -10\right\}$
192. $\left\{-\dfrac{15}{7}, 3\right\}$
193. $\{-12, 20\}$
194. $\left\{2, -\dfrac{2}{5}\right\}$
195. $\left\{-\dfrac{1}{2}, -2\right\}$
196. $\left\{-7, \dfrac{23}{2}\right\}$
197. $\left\{6, -\dfrac{46}{7}\right\}$
198. $\{1, 3\}$
199. $\{2, -3\}$
200. $\{6, 2\}$
201. $\{-11, 5\}$
202. $\{-20, 28\}$
203. $\{7, -4\}$
204. $\{1, 3\}$
205. $\left\{\dfrac{13}{5}, -5\right\}$
206. $\left\{-3, \dfrac{7}{5}\right\}$
207. $\left\{\dfrac{23}{3}, -9\right\}$
208. $\{7, -1\}$
209. $\left\{\dfrac{51}{7}, -9\right\}$

210. $\{5, -8\}$

211. $\left\{-9, \dfrac{31}{3}\right\}$

212. $\left\{\dfrac{8}{5}, -4\right\}$

213. $\left\{9, -\dfrac{23}{3}\right\}$

214. $\{-5, 3\}$

215. $\{-4, 1\}$

216. $\left\{7, -\dfrac{51}{5}\right\}$

217. $\{-2, -4\}$

218. $\left\{\dfrac{1}{4}, \dfrac{9}{4}\right\}$

219. $\{3, -11\}$

220. $\left\{\dfrac{41}{6}, \dfrac{13}{2}\right\}$

221. $\left\{-\dfrac{17}{8}, \dfrac{7}{8}\right\}$

222. $\left\{-5, \dfrac{20}{3}\right\}$

223. $\left\{\dfrac{19}{3}, -3\right\}$

224. $\left\{-\dfrac{5}{3}, \dfrac{11}{3}\right\}$

225. $\{-4, 10\}$

226. $\{15, -9\}$

227. $\{-9, -3\}$

228. $\{-7, -9\}$

229. $\left\{-\dfrac{23}{4}, 7\right\}$

230. $\left\{\dfrac{47}{7}, -9\right\}$

231. $\left\{10, -\dfrac{50}{3}\right\}$

232. $\left\{\dfrac{66}{5}, -10\right\}$

233. $\left\{\dfrac{5}{2}, -\dfrac{7}{2}\right\}$

234. $\left\{\dfrac{39}{4}, -9\right\}$

235. $\left\{\dfrac{28}{3}, -8\right\}$

236. $\left\{6, -\dfrac{12}{5}\right\}$

237. $\left\{9, -\dfrac{41}{4}\right\}$

238. $\left\{\dfrac{14}{5}, -\dfrac{2}{5}\right\}$

239. $\{6, 3\}$

240. $\left\{\dfrac{53}{5}, -9\right\}$

241. $\left\{-\dfrac{8}{5}, \dfrac{4}{5}\right\}$

242. $\left\{\dfrac{4}{3}, -1\right\}$

243. $\{1, -4\}$

244. $\{-8, 9\}$

245. $\left\{-\dfrac{9}{2}, 3\right\}$

246. $\left\{\dfrac{17}{7}, \dfrac{37}{7}\right\}$

247. $\left\{\dfrac{1}{4}, \dfrac{11}{4}\right\}$

248. $\left\{1, \dfrac{7}{5}\right\}$

249. $\left\{-\dfrac{34}{5}, \dfrac{26}{5}\right\}$

250. $\left\{\dfrac{32}{5}, -6\right\}$

251. $\{11, -8\}$

252. $\left\{5, -\dfrac{7}{2}\right\}$

253. $\left\{4, -\dfrac{10}{7}\right\}$

254. $\left\{\dfrac{1}{5}, -1\right\}$

255. $\left\{7, -\dfrac{17}{5}\right\}$

256. $\left\{-1, -\dfrac{13}{3}\right\}$

257. $\left\{0, -\dfrac{8}{5}\right\}$

258. $\{4, -3\}$

259. $\left\{\dfrac{24}{5}, -3\right\}$

260. $\{17, -9\}$

261. $\left\{-9, \dfrac{9}{2}\right\}$

262. $\left\{-\dfrac{9}{2}, 4\right\}$

263. $\{18, -6\}$

264. $\left\{-8, \dfrac{4}{3}\right\}$

265. $\left\{\dfrac{13}{2}, -4\right\}$

266. $\left\{-\dfrac{13}{3}, -\dfrac{5}{3}\right\}$

267. $\left\{2, -\dfrac{3}{5}\right\}$

268. $\left\{\dfrac{13}{3}, -2\right\}$

269. $\left\{\dfrac{4}{9}, -\dfrac{20}{9}\right\}$

270. $\left\{\dfrac{5}{4}, -\dfrac{25}{4}\right\}$

271. $\left\{6, -\dfrac{11}{3}\right\}$

272. $\{13, -4\}$

273. $\left\{-\dfrac{26}{7}, 4\right\}$

274. $\{3, 0\}$

275. $\left\{-\dfrac{21}{10}, \dfrac{3}{10}\right\}$

276. $\{0, 4\}$

277. $\left\{4, -\dfrac{20}{3}\right\}$

278. $\left\{-7, \dfrac{47}{5}\right\}$

279. $\left\{2, -\dfrac{13}{3}\right\}$

280. $\left\{3, -\dfrac{27}{5}\right\}$

281. $\left\{\dfrac{29}{9}, -5\right\}$

282. $\{-1, -3\}$

283. $\left\{\dfrac{15}{7}, -\dfrac{25}{7}\right\}$

284. $\left\{-\dfrac{19}{5}, 2\right\}$

285. $\{4, 6\}$

286. $\{-8, 4\}$

287. $\left\{10, -\dfrac{94}{9}\right\}$

288. $\{4, 0\}$

289. $\left\{\dfrac{1}{5}, -2\right\}$

290. $\{7, -1\}$

291. $\{11, -9\}$

292. $\{6, 3\}$

293. $\left\{\dfrac{7}{2}, -6\right\}$

294. $\left\{\dfrac{13}{5}, -3\right\}$

295. $\left\{\dfrac{27}{5}, -6\right\}$

296. $\{-1, -5\}$

297. $\left\{\dfrac{13}{2}, -\dfrac{11}{2}\right\}$

298. $\{-2, -8\}$

299. $\left\{-4, \dfrac{4}{3}\right\}$

300. $\left\{\dfrac{18}{5}, -\dfrac{32}{5}\right\}$

Chapter 4: Quadratic equations

1. $\{-1, -9\}$
2. $\{3, -13\}$
3. $\{14, 4\}$
4. $\{12, 4\}$
5. $\{11, 5\}$
6. $\{1, -7\}$
7. $\{2, -4\}$
8. $\{20, -2\}$
9. $\{19, -3\}$
10. $\{3, -15\}$
11. $\{-3, -9\}$
12. $\{11, 7\}$
13. $\{8, -4\}$
14. $\{-5, -9\}$
15. $\{13, 3\}$
16. $\{5, -7\}$
17. $\{-5, -11\}$
18. $\{16, -4\}$
19. $\{6, -16\}$
20. $\{-2, -18\}$
21. $\{16, -2\}$
22. $\{19, -1\}$
23. $\{8, 4\}$
24. $\{14, -6\}$
25. $\{11, -9\}$
26. $\{11, -5\}$
27. $\{3, -17\}$
28. $\{6, -8\}$
29. $\{-3, -5\}$
30. $\{-4, -6\}$
31. $\{-4, -8\}$
32. $\{22, -4\}$
33. $\{1, -21\}$
34. $\{5, -19\}$
35. $\{9, -5\}$
36. $\{12, -6\}$
37. $\{3, -11\}$
38. $\{-1, -11\}$
39. $\{3, -21\}$
40. $\{12, -2\}$
41. $\{9, -3\}$
42. $\{12, 2\}$
43. $\{6, -4\}$
44. $\{13, -7\}$
45. $\{20, -4\}$
46. $\{-7, -9\}$
47. $\{14, 2\}$
48. $\{5, -1\}$
49. $\{16, 2\}$
50. $\{6, 2\}$
51. $\{-4, -14\}$
52. $\{-3, -13\}$
53. $\{5, -3\}$
54. $\{11, 9\}$
55. $\{8, 6\}$
56. $\{-7, -11\}$
57. $\{9, 7\}$
58. $\{6, -10\}$
59. $\{4, -12\}$
60. $\{16, -6\}$
61. $\{-2, -8\}$
62. $\{15, -5\}$
63. $\{13, -3\}$
64. $\{24, -4\}$
65. $\{5, -15\}$
66. $\{2, -10\}$
67. $\{18, -4\}$
68. $\{5, -17\}$
69. $\{1, -19\}$
70. $\{11, -3\}$
71. $\{7, -9\}$
72. $\{-8, -10\}$
73. $\{13, -1\}$
74. $\{23, -3\}$
75. $\{4, 2\}$
76. $\{15, 3\}$
77. $\{11, 3\}$

78. {-1, -7}
79. {18, 2}
80. {7, -13}
81. {8, -12}
82. {9, 1}
83. {2, -16}
84. {2, -12}
85. {15, -3}
86. {-4, -10}
87. {-2, -4}
88. {5, -13}
89. {-4, -16}
90. {-6, -12}
91. {-5, -13}
92. {4, -14}
93. {-6, -8}
94. {1, -15}
95. {7, -5}
96. {2, -14}
97. {-6, -10}
98. {6, -14}
99. {-2, -12}
100. {-1, -9}
101. {15, -5}
102. {4, -18}
103. {12, -8}
104. {1, -9}
105. {-1, -13}
106. {6, -14}
107. {6, -8}
108. {4, -10}
109. {4, -22}

110. {-3, -7}
111. {7, 1}
112. {13, -5}
113. {17, 1}
114. {-5, -15}
115. {-2, -14}
116. {17, -5}
117. {23, -3}
118. {9, 5}
119. {8, -4}
120. {12, 2}
121. {8, -10}
122. {2, -8}
123. {-2, -16}
124. {12, 4}
125. {3, -13}
126. {7, -9}
127. {2, -16}
128. {7, -13}
129. {5, -9}
130. {2, -20}
131. {-6, -8}
132. {-7, -9}
133. {-5, -7}
134. {-1, -17}
135. {-2, -12}
136. {3, 1}
137. {9, -5}
138. {8, 4}
139. {1, -7}
140. {17, -3}
141. {5, -1}

142. {10, 6}
143. {5, -15}
144. {7, -3}
145. {15, -1}
146. {-1, -3}
147. {-4, -10}
148. {6, -2}
149. {21, -1}
150. {19, -1}
151. {-3, -17}
152. {4, -2}
153. {-3, -15}
154. {11, 1}
155. {10, 2}
156. {8, -6}
157. {-5, -11}
158. {11, -5}
159. {1, -13}
160. {2, -4}
161. {3, -19}
162. {10, 8}
163. {9, 3}
164. {8, 2}
165. {10, -8}
166. {7, 5}
167. {6, -12}
168. {6, -16}
169. {15, 5}
170. {13, -1}
171. {10, -6}
172. {14, 4}
173. {24, -4}

174. {-1, -19}
175. {6, -10}
176. {-2, -4}
177. {6, 2}
178. {-4, -14}
179. {1, -3}
180. {18, 2}
181. {7, -1}
182. {8, 6}
183. {-2, -6}
184. {6, 4}
185. {1, -21}
186. {11, -1}
187. {4, -24}
188. {18, -4}
189. {-1, -5}
190. {-7, -11}
191. {-3, -11}
192. {4, -12}
193. {13, -7}
194. {9, 7}
195. {-2, -18}
196. {5, 1}
197. {-5, -13}
198. {10, -2}
199. {6, -14}
200. {13, -1}
201. {7, 5}
202. {1, -21}
203. {-2, -10}
204. {3, -17}
205. {17, -1}

206. {20, -4}
207. {12, -4}
208. {17, -5}
209. {12, 2}
210. {6, 2}
211. {15, 3}
212. {9, -5}
213. {5, -17}
214. {5, -3}
215. {5, -11}
216. {3, -11}
217. {10, -6}
218. {-5, -13}
219. {-2, -8}
220. {19, -1}
221. {15, -5}
222. {21, -3}
223. {8, -10}
224. {9, 5}
225. {4, -16}
226. {11, 3}
227. {8, 2}
228. {-2, -18}
229. {5, -1}
230. {7, -3}
231. {2, -12}
232. {10, -8}
233. {-5, -11}
234. {7, -1}
235. {-3, -5}
236. {12, -2}
237. {-1, -15}

238. {-1, -5}
239. {-5, -7}
240. {-6, -8}
241. {12, 6}
242. {-4, -10}
243. {10, 6}
244. {7, -5}
245. {2, -10}
246. {1, -13}
247. {-2, -6}
248. {15, -3}
249. {10, 8}
250. {13, 3}
251. {-1, -13}
252. {-7, -11}
253. {-7, -9}
254. {8, 6}
255. {15, 1}
256. {13, -5}
257. {-1, -3}
258. {14, -4}
259. {1, -9}
260. {-3, -11}
261. {-3, -15}
262. {5, -15}
263. {-2, -14}
264. {14, -2}
265. {12, -8}
266. {-2, -12}
267. {8, -12}
268. {-8, -12}
269. {-7, -13}

270. {3, 1}
271. {7, -9}
272. {11, -1}
273. {-4, -8}
274. {2, -8}
275. {6, -8}
276. {6, -10}
277. {3, -13}
278. {10, 2}
279. {6, -12}
280. {5, 1}
281. {-1, -7}
282. {7, -13}
283. {9, -11}
284. {10, 4}
285. {11, 1}
286. {2, -16}
287. {-5, -15}
288. {13, 1}
289. {-1, -9}
290. {1, -19}
291. {6, -16}
292. {14, -6}
293. {8, -4}
294. {8, -2}
295. {-1, -11}
296. {2, -4}
297. {1, -15}
298. {11, 3}
299. {3, -21}
300. {-3, -15}

Chapter 5: Solving Quadratic Equation using the Formula

1. {8, -10}
2. {11, -8}
3. $\{2\frac{2}{3}, -2\}$
4. {6, -8}
5. {5, -8}
6. {-3, -9}
7. {5, -6}
8. {5, -12}
9. {9, 2}
10. {16, -8}
11. {12, -5}
12. $\{2, \frac{1}{2}\}$
13. {11, -3}
14. {6, -3}
15. {12, -8}
16. $\{2\frac{1}{4}, -4\}$
17. {10, -8}
18. {7, -19}
19. {12, -2}
20. $\{\frac{1}{4}, -1\}$
21. {7, -4}
22. $\{-\frac{1}{2}, -5\}$
23. {6, 3}
24. {4, -1}
25. {5, 3}
26. {8, -7}
27. {4, -2}
28. {6, -2}
29. $\{3\frac{2}{3}, -4\}$
30. {1, -11}
31. $\{1, \frac{1}{5}\}$
32. {3, -2}
33. {4, -1}
34. {5, -2}
35. {11, -6}
36. {1, -2}
37. $\{3, -\frac{1}{2}\}$
38. {11, -9}
39. {-1, -6}
40. {5, -13}
41. {4, -9}
42. {3, -6}
43. {7, -16}
44. {11, -6}
45. {5, -11}
46. {2, -9}
47. {2, -4}
48. $\{\frac{1}{2}, -\frac{1}{3}\}$
49. {2, -3}
50. {6, -4}
51. {7, -6}
52. {6, -2}
53. {4, -6}
54. $\{3, -1\frac{2}{3}\}$
55. {5, -4}
56. $\{4\frac{1}{2}, -4\frac{2}{3}\}$
57. $\{4, -3\frac{1}{2}\}$
58. {5, -1}
59. $\{9, -7\frac{1}{2}\}$
60. $\{3, -2\frac{1}{4}\}$
61. $\{4, -3\frac{3}{5}\}$
62. $\{4\frac{4}{5}, -6\}$
63. $\{2\frac{1}{2}, -\frac{2}{3}\}$
64. $\{2\frac{1}{2}, -1\}$
65. $\{2\frac{3}{5}, -1\}$
66. $\{6, -4\frac{1}{3}\}$
67. $\{4, -5\frac{2}{3}\}$
68. $\{2, -2\frac{5}{6}\}$
69. $\{3\frac{1}{2}, -3\}$
70. {-1, -5}
71. $\{3\frac{1}{2}, -9\}$
72. {-2, -3}
73. $\{3, -4\frac{3}{4}\}$
74. {8, -11}
75. $\{2, -3\frac{2}{5}\}$
76. $\{7, -6\frac{2}{3}\}$
77. $\{2\frac{1}{2}, -2\}$
78. {3, -4}
79. {8, -4}
80. $\{2\frac{1}{2}, 1\}$
81. $\{4\frac{4}{5}, -5\}$
82. $\{8, -4\frac{2}{3}\}$
83. $\{1\frac{1}{2}, -6\}$
84. $\{1\frac{2}{3}, -1\frac{1}{2}\}$
85. $\{1\frac{2}{5}, -1\}$
86. $\{4, -4\frac{1}{2}\}$
87. $\{7\frac{1}{2}, -8\}$
88. $\{3\frac{2}{5}, -2\}$
89. {7, -14}
90. $\{\frac{2}{3}, -3\}$
91. {3, -7}
92. $\{6, -3\frac{4}{5}\}$
93. {13, -10}
94. {3, -2}
95. $\{3, -\frac{4}{5}\}$
96. $\{3, -1\frac{1}{6}\}$
97. $\{5, -3\frac{3}{5}\}$
98. {4, -8}
99. {8, -12}
100. $\{6\frac{1}{3}, -5\}$

Chapter 6: Systems of Linear Equations

1. (-3, 4)
2. (4, -2)
3. (9, 4)
4. (-3, -5)
5. (4, 4)
6. (-3, 2)
7. (9, -6)
8. (-2, -2)
9. (-1, 5)
10. (-5, -3)
11. (-2, -6)
12. (9, -8)
13. (-5, -2)
14. (2, 2)
15. (1, -6)
16. (9, -4)
17. (-3, -6)
18. (6, -4)
19. (8, -8)
20. (3, -2)
21. (2, -3)
22. (9, -3)
23. (-1, -5)
24. (5, 3)
25. (-3, -1)
26. (4, -9)
27. (7, 6)
28. (-4, 2)
29. (4, 5)
30. (6, -5)
31. (-7, 8)
32. (8, -9)
33. (8, 6)
34. (2, -1)
35. (5, 8)
36. (6, -8)
37. (6, 2)
38. (1, 1)
39. (-9, 6)
40. (2, 3)
41. (-9, 2)
42. (-5, -6)
43. (8, 4)
44. (7, -2)
45. (-6, -1)
46. (-7, -1)
47. (1, 4)
48. (6, -3)
49. (-1, -5)
50. (1, -2)
51. (1, -4)
52. (-8, 1)
53. (-5, -8)
54. (-3, 8)
55. (4, -9)
56. (7, -9)
57. (9, 1)
58. (-9, 3)
59. (2, 8)
60. (3, -2)
61. (-6, 5)
62. (6, 3)
63. (4, 5)
64. (-8, 6)
65. (-1, 8)
66. (-6, -6)
67. (-8, 7)
68. (-4, 9)
69. (-6, -8)
70. (-6, -7)
71. (1, -5)
72. (1, -2)
73. (-8, 3)
74. (-9, -9)
75. (1, 2)
76. (-1, 4)
77. (-3, -3)
78. (9, 5)
79. (-9, -9)

80. (-4, 2)
81. (3, -6)
82. (7, 7)
83. (3, 1)
84. (5, -8)
85. (9, -7)
86. (1, -6)
87. (-5, 1)
88. (-1, 4)
89. (-7, -3)
90. (5, -7)
91. (4, 8)
92. (1, 2)
93. (-1, -2)
94. (7, -5)
95. (4, 9)
96. (7, -4)
97. (9, -5)
98. (6, 5)
99. (2, 2)
100. (8, -9)
101. (4, 8)
102. (4, 4)
103. (9, -5)
104. (-5, 9)
105. (-8, 9)
106. (6, 2)
107. (-4, 5)
108. (1, 6)
109. (-9, -4)
110. (-1, 8)
111. (-1, 9)
112. (-1, 4)
113. (1, -8)
114. (8, -1)

115. (5, 3)
116. (8, -7)
117. (6, 6)
118. (-1, 2)
119. (-3, 7)
120. (-3, 8)
121. (-6, 9)
122. (1, 5)
123. (7, 2)
124. (-9, 6)
125. (2, 2)
126. (5, 9)
127. (7, 6)
128. (2, 7)
129. (6, 6)
130. (-7, -1)
131. (-1, -1)
132. (-3, 1)
133. (-5, 4)
134. (6, 1)
135. (4, -4)
136. (3, -7)
137. (3, 2)
138. (6, 1)
139. (5, 1)
140. (6, 4)
141. (-4, 4)
142. (-1, 3)
143. (1, 2)
144. (1, 5)
145. (9, -1)
146. (6, -8)
147. (-3, -6)
148. (6, 6)
149. (6, -2)

150. (-1, 1)
151. (-9, 8)
152. (-8, 1)
153. (8, -5)
154. (9, -1)
155. (4, -6)
156. (3, -6)
157. (-5, -2)
158. (9, -1)
159. (-9, -5)
160. (7, -3)
161. (1, -2)
162. (-3, -2)
163. (9, 6)
164. (-8, -6)
165. (3, 4)
166. (5, 8)
167. (-3, -6)
168. (3, -6)
169. (8, -1)
170. (5, 8)
171. (-7, 4)
172. (5, -4)
173. (2, 9)
174. (-2, -3)
175. (1, 5)
176. (3, 7)
177. (4, 6)
178. (9, -3)
179. (-2, 2)
180. (-3, -5)
181. (-6, -3)
182. (9, 1)
183. (4, -9)
184. (5, -7)

185. (4, 1)
186. (3, 8)
187. (9, 5)
188. (8, -5)
189. (-6, -8)
190. (3, -3)
191. (-4, 1)
192. (-7, 1)
193. (-8, 9)
194. (-9, -9)
195. (-6, -9)
196. (-2, 3)
197. (8, -6)
198. (4, -3)
199. (4, 6)
200. (7, 1)
201. (2, -2)
202. (-8, 8)
203. (-7, 9)
204. (-5, -7)
205. (-8, -8)
206. (-4, -2)
207. (-5, -2)
208. (4, 7)
209. (-7, -8)
210. (2, 5)
211. (9, -7)
212. (-3, -7)
213. (3, -5)
214. (2, -6)
215. (3, -2)
216. (3, -3)
217. (1, -7)
218. (4, 6)
219. (-6, -3)

220. (1, 7)
221. (2, 8)
222. (-9, -4)
223. (4, 1)
224. (-1, 8)
225. (3, -5)
226. (2, 1)
227. (2, -6)
228. (-2, 3)
229. (1, 4)
230. (-6, 1)
231. (-1, -1)
232. (8, 2)
233. (9, 6)
234. (2, -5)
235. (4, -2)
236. (-6, -4)
237. (3, 7)
238. (-2, 1)
239. (-7, -1)
240. (2, 6)
241. (-1, 9)
242. (7, 8)
243. (8, 8)
244. (-7, 7)
245. (5, -4)
246. (-6, -6)
247. (-9, -2)
248. (-3, -9)
249. (4, 7)
250. (6, -7)
251. (-8, 9)
252. (-5, -4)
253. (4, 9)
254. (-3, -1)

255. (5, -2)
256. (-2, 1)
257. (8, 9)
258. (-2, -2)
259. (2, 3)
260. (6, -1)
261. (-1, -6)
262. (-8, 9)
263. (-7, -2)
264. (8, -3)
265. (2, 9)
266. (5, -5)
267. (7, -9)
268. (3, 9)
269. (-1, 9)
270. (-3, 3)
271. (3, 2)
272. (-6, 5)
273. (-2, 2)
274. (-4, 4)
275. (-3, -8)
276. (2, 8)
277. (7, -1)
278. (-2, 9)
279. (-9, 3)
280. (8, -3)
281. (-9, 1)
282. (8, 1)
283. (-6, -3)
284. (-9, -9)
285. (9, -6)
286. (5, 6)
287. (-6, -2)
288. (4, 9)
289. (3, 2)

290. (-6, -2)
291. (-5, -3)
292. (-2, 7)
293. (7, -4)
294. (-6, 1)
295. (1, -4)
296. (6, -8)